DATE DUE

BRODART, CO. Cat. No. 23-221-003

Careers in Focus

Transportation

Ferguson Publishing Company
Chicago, Illinois

Copyright © 2000 Ferguson Publishing Company
ISBN 0-89434-317-3

Printed in the United States of America

Cover photo courtesy Tony Stone Images

Published and distributed by
Ferguson Publishing Company
200 West Jackson, 7th Floor
Chicago, Illinois 60606
800-306-9941
www.fergpubco.com

All rights reserved. No part of this publication may be reproduced, stored in a retrieval system, or transmitted by any means, electronic, mechanical, photocopying or otherwise, without the prior permission of the publisher.

X-3

Table of Contents

Introduction

Transportation is a massive field incorporating air, rail, road, and water travel. Moving freight from producers and manufacturers to consumers is as big a part of the industry as personal travel—and freight, too, may be transported by airplane, train, truck, or ship.

Each branch of the transportation industry requires workers in a variety of positions, from managers who coordinate shipping schedules to freighthandlers and customer service representatives. Many workers are needed just to operate the various means of transportation, such as bus drivers and airplane pilots.

Transportation is an ever-expanding industry, with increasingly efficient vehicles and the growing public desire to travel spurring it on. Job opportunities are, therefore, generally quite good, and employees' prospects are stable. Advances in transportation technology may eliminate some jobs, but they also create more employment opportunities for people with technological training.

Many airlines are once again enjoying increased profits. The number of passengers flying each year is increasing and is expected to increase into the next century. However, fewer airlines are operating than before, and more mergers and consolidations among airlines can be expected in the future. Fare wars among airlines competing for passengers have reduced the profit margins. Airlines, like most corporations, will need to do more with fewer resources and find new ways of making their operations more efficient. Growth in the airline industry has slowed; employment across the industry is down. Overall, however, many in the airline industry are predicting that the number of flights will grow by 60 percent over the next ten years and the number of passengers will pass 800 million each year. If these predictions hold true, employment in the airline industry will have to grow, too.

Most railroads expect to continue streamlining their operations, as technological innovations take the place of human labor. While this is clearly beneficial for the industry itself, it unfortunately does not indicate a good outlook for railroad job-seekers. The federal Bureau of Labor Statistics predicts a decline in railroad transportation positions overall, with only small increases expected in a few job categories through 2006, including locomotive engineers and subway and streetcar operators. Subway and streetcar employment is expected to grow as large cities add new lines and commuters turn to rail to escape congested highways.

The number of jobs in the trucking industry is expected to grow as fast as the average through 2006. Administrative, dispatch, and material handling positions are expected to grow as fast as the average. Certain other sectors of the industry are expected to have an above-average number of job openings, especially drivers and mechanics. The generally strong U.S. economy has produced a tight labor market and many truck companies are finding it difficult to attract and keep qualified drivers. There is a considerable amount of turnover in the field and beginners are able to find many openings. Competition is expected to remain strong for the more desirable jobs, such as those with large companies or the easiest routes.

Shipping is not considered a growth industry in terms of employment. The industry is stable, and it is expected that job opportunities will remain good but limited. According to U.S. government predictions, there will be, at best, a 10 percent increase in available jobs between 1995 and 2006. In fact, as of 1996, the total number of employees in the water transportation industry in the 1990s had slowly and steadily decreased, according to the U.S. Department of Transportation. Pressure is on to increase productivity through automation, which translates into fewer employment opportunities. This is especially true for many of the clerical positions, as more and more computers are used to store and retrieve information.

Each article in this book discusses a particular transportation occupation in detail. The information comes from Ferguson's *Encyclopedia of Careers and Vocational Guidance*. The History section describes the history of the particular job as it relates to the overall development of its industry or field. The Job describes the primary and secondary duties of the job. Requirements discusses high school and postsecondary education and training requirements, any certification or licensing necessary, and any other personal requirements for success in the job. Exploring offers suggestions on how to gain some experience in or knowledge of the particular job before making a firm educational and financial commitment. The focus is on what can be done while still in high school (or in the early years of college) to gain a better understanding of the job. The Employers section gives an overview of typical places of employment for the job. Starting Out discusses the best ways to land that first job, be it through the college placement office, newspaper ads, or personal contact. The Advancement section describes what kind of career path to expect from the job and how to get there. Earnings lists salary ranges and describes the typical fringe benefits. The Work Environment section describes the typical surroundings and conditions of employment—whether indoors or outdoors, noisy or quiet, social or independent, and so on. Also discussed are typical hours worked, any seasonal fluctuations, and the stresses and strains of the job. The Outlook section summarizes the job in terms of the general economy and industry projections. For the most part, Outlook information is obtained from the Bureau of Labor Statistics and is supplemented by information taken from professional associations. Job growth terms follow those used in the *Occupational Outlook Handbook:*

- Growth described as "much faster than the average" means an increase of 36 percent or more.
- Growth described as "faster than the average" means an increase of 21 to 35 percent.
- Growth described as "about as fast as the average" means an increase of 10 to 20 percent.
- Growth described as "little change or more slowly than the average" means an increase of 0 to 9 percent.
- "Decline" means a decrease of 1 percent or more.

Each article ends with For More Information, which lists organizations that can provide career information on training, education, internships, scholarships, and job placement.

Air Traffic Controllers

School Subjects

Computer science
Geography

Personal Skills

Leadership/management
Technical/scientific

Work Environment

Primarily indoors
Primarily one location

Minimum Education Level

Bachelor's degree

Salary Range

$24,178 to $57,000 to $100,000

Certification or Licensing

Required by all states

Outlook

Decline

Overview

Air traffic controllers monitor and direct the activities of aircraft into and out of airports and along specified flight routes. They radio pilots with approach, landing, taxiing, and takeoff instructions, and advisories on weather and other conditions in order to maintain the safe and orderly flow of air traffic both in the air and on the ground.

History

The goal of the first air traffic control efforts—beacon lights—was to guide airplanes along a specified airway. As airways and aircraft grew in number, radio communication and radio beacons were added to help planes navigate and to provide weather forecasts. In 1936, the federal government opened the first air traffic control center to regulate the increasing numbers of aircraft flying into and out of the country's growing airports. The Instrument Landing System, a method for signaling aircraft, was instituted in 1941.

Airplanes were reaching higher speeds and altitudes, and the controllers' functions became more important to guard against collisions, to ensure safe landings, and to warn pilots of potential weather and geographic hazards in flights. Radar, developed during World War II, allowed air traffic controllers to track the movements of many aircraft and for longer distances. The air traffic control network was extended to include centers at airports, en route, and flight service stations, each of which performed specific tasks and controlled specific portions of the skies. After the war, more sophisticated communication systems were developed, including VOR (very high frequency omnidirectional range) transmission, which was used to signal flight path data directly to the plane. Computers were soon installed in order to provide still greater accuracy to the air traffic controller's instructions. Development of the Global Positioning System (GPS), however, has made it possible for airplanes to achieve greater control over their flight paths, so fewer air traffic controllers will be needed to protect the skies.

The Job

Air traffic controllers work in one of three areas: airport traffic control towers, en route air traffic control centers, or flight service stations. The Federal Aviation Administration (FAA), which regulates all air traffic, employs almost every air traffic controller in the United States. Some private airports employ their own air traffic controllers; others are employed at military airports.

Terminal air traffic control specialists are stationed in airport control towers and are responsible for all air traffic entering, leaving, or passing through the airspace around the airport, as well as conducting airplane traffic on the ground. These controllers use radar and visual observation to maintain safe distances among aircraft, and they provide information on weather and other conditions to the pilots under their control. As an airplane prepares for departure, the ground controller issues taxiing instructions to bring it to the runway. A local controller contacts the pilot with weather, wind, speed, and visibility conditions and clears the pilot for takeoff. A departure controller monitors the aircraft on radar, maintains radio contact with the pilot until the aircraft has left the airport's airspace, and hands over control of the plane to an en route control center. A radar controller monitors the traffic above the airport and into the aircraft's flight route, communicating with the other controllers. Approaching aircraft are handled in a reverse procedure. When many aircraft are approaching the airport at the same time, the controllers arrange them in a holding pattern above the airport until they each can be cleared to land.

There are more than 440 air traffic control towers in airports across the country. At a small airport, an air traffic controller may be expected to perform all of these functions. Controllers at larger airports usually specialize in a single area. *Senior controllers* supervise the activities of the entire center. *Terminal air traffic controllers* may be responsible for all aircraft within as much as a 50-mile radius of their airport. Most controllers are responsible for many aircraft at once; they track their positions on the radar screen, receive instrument flight data such as an airplane's speed and altitude, coordinate the altitudes at which planes within the area will fly, keep track of weather conditions, and maintain constant communication with the pilots and with controllers at their and other control centers. An air traffic controller must be aware of all of the activities in the air traffic control center and around the airport. When an aircraft experiences an emergency, air traffic controllers must respond quickly, clearing a path for that aircraft through the traffic, alerting fire and rescue teams, and guiding the pilot to a safe landing.

En route air traffic control specialists work at one of 20 regional centers in the United States. They coordinate the movements of aircraft between airports but out of range of the airport traffic controllers. Because an en route center may be responsible for many thousands of square miles of airspace, these controllers generally work in teams of two or three, with each team assigned a particular section of the center's airspace. Each team consists of a radar controller, the senior member of the team, and radar associates. A center may employ as many as 700 controllers and have 150 or more on duty during peak flying hours. Within the center's airspace are designated routes that the aircraft fly. En route controllers monitor traffic along those air routes. They use radar and electronic equipment to track the flights within the center's airspace and to maintain contact with planes within their area, giving instructions, air traffic clearances, and advice about flight conditions. If flight plans for two airplanes conflict, the en route team will contact the team responsible for the preceding section in order to change one plane's flight path. The controllers will also coordinate changes in altitudes and speeds among pilots. En route controllers receive or transfer control of the aircraft to controllers in adjacent centers or to an airport's approach controller as the craft enters that facility's airspace.

Flight service station air traffic control specialists make up the third group of controllers. They provide preflight or inflight assistance to pilots from more than 125 flight service stations linked by a broad communications system. These controllers give pilots information about the station's particular area, including terrain, weather, and anything else necessary to guarantee a safe flight. They may suggest alternate routes or different altitudes, alert pilots to military operations taking place along certain routes, inform them about landing at airports that have no towers, assist pilots in emergency situations, and participate in searches for missing or overdue aircraft.

Requirements

High School

Because all air traffic controllers must have a college degree, high school students interested in the field must pursue a college-prep curriculum. Mathematics and science courses are especially useful courses to study because they are most directly related to air traffic control work.

Postsecondary Training

Trainees for air traffic control positions must have completed four years of college or have three years of work experience or a combination of both; entry to civil aviation is also possible through the military. Trainees are selected from applicants who receive a high score on the federal civil service examination. The written test measures aptitudes for arithmetic, abstract reasoning, three-dimensional spatial visualization, and other indicators of an ability to learn the controller's duties.

Following the civil service test, the highest scoring applicants are next subjected to an intensive one-week screening in an effort to determine if the candidates have the required alertness, decisiveness, motivation, poise, and ability to work under extreme pressure. This screening consists of an aptitude test, computer simulations, as well as physical and mental health examinations.

Those accepted into the training program receive 11 to 17 weeks of intensive instruction at the FAA Academy in Oklahoma City. There they receive training in the fundamentals of the airway systems, civil air regulations, radar, and aircraft performance characteristics. They practice on machines designed to simulate emergency situations to determine their emotional stability under pressure. The standards for those who successfully complete this program are very high; about 50 percent of the trainees are dropped during this period. Those who complete the program are guaranteed jobs with the FAA.

Certification or Licensing

Training continues on the job, and new controllers also receive classroom instruction. Depending on the size and complexity of the facility, a new hire may require between 18 months and three years to become a fully certified air traffic controller. Controllers must be certified at each progressive level of air traffic control, usually within a certain period of time. Failure to be certified within the time limit is grounds for dismissal. Air traffic controllers are also required to pass annual physical exams and performance reviews.

Other Requirements

Applicants for airport tower or en route traffic control jobs must be under 31 years of age, pass physical and psychological examinations, and have vision that is or can be corrected to 20/20. Flight service stations will accept applicants over the age of 31. Persons hoping to enter the field must be articulate, have a good memory, and show self-control. It is imperative that they be able to express themselves clearly, remember rapidly changing data that affect their decisions, and be able to operate calmly under very difficult situations involving a great deal of strain. They must also be able to make good, sound, and quickly derived decisions. A poor decision may mean the loss of a large number of lives.

Exploring

Many air traffic control centers welcome and encourage visits from high school students and others interested in this career. Talking with air traffic controllers and watching them work will provide a strong introduction to their day-to-day activities. Speaking with aircraft pilots may provide other insights into the role of the air traffic controller. Visits and interviews can be arranged through most airports, air traffic control centers, the Air Traffic Control Association, and many airlines. Students interested in this career will also find that every branch of the military services offers opportunities for experience in these and related jobs.

Employers

Air traffic controllers are employed only by the Federal Aviation Administration.

Starting Out

The first step in becoming an air traffic controller starts with the written civil service exam, followed by the one-week screening. Acceptance is on a highly competitive basis. High grades in college or strong work experience is considered essential. Experience in related fields, including those of pilots, air dispatch operators, and other positions with either the civil airlines or the military service, will be important for those with and especially for those without a college degree. Actual air control experience gained in military service may be a plus. However, civil aviation rules are quite different from military aviation rules. Because the FAA provides complete training, applicants with strong skills and abilities in abstract reasoning, communication, and problem-solving, as well as the ability to learn and to work independently, will have the best chance of entering this field.

Advancement

After becoming a controller, those who do particularly well may reach the level of supervisor or manager. Many others advance to even more responsible positions in air control, and some might move into the top administrative jobs with the FAA. Competitive civil service status can be earned at the end of one year on the job, and career status after the satisfactory completion of three years of work in the area.

In the case of both airport control specialists and en route control specialists, the responsibilities become more complex with each successive promotion. Controllers generally begin at the GS-7 level and advance by completing certification requirements for the different air traffic control specialists. New hires at an airport control tower usually begin by communicating flight data and airport conditions to pilots before progressing through the ranks of ground controller, local controller, departure controller, and, lastly, arrival controller. At an en route center, trainees begin by processing flight plans, then advance to become radar associate controllers, and, finally, radar controllers.

After becoming fully qualified, controllers who exhibit strong management, organizational, and job skills may advance to become area supervisors and managers and control tower or flight service station managers. Employees in the higher grades may be responsible for a number of different areas, including the coordination of the traffic control activities within the control area, the supervision and training of en route traffic controllers or airport traffic controllers in lower positions, and management in various aeronautical agencies. These positions generally become available after three to five years of fully qualified service.

Earnings

In 1997, trainees started at about $24,178 a year. The average salary for all controllers was $46,000 per year. At the highest grade, GS-14, salaries ranged from $57,000 to $75,000 per year. Controllers with a great deal of seniority and those at the nation's busiest airports can earn more than $100,000 per year in wages, overtime, and benefits. Controllers may also earn bonuses based on performance.

Because of the complexity of their job duties and the tension involved in their work, air traffic controllers are offered better benefits than other federal employees. Depending on their length of service, air traffic controllers receive 13 to 26 days of paid vacation and 13 days of paid sick leave per year, plus life insurance and health benefits. Controllers also receive 10 or more paid federal holidays. In addition, they are permitted to retire earlier and with fewer years of service than other federal employees. An air traffic controller with 20 years' experience may retire at the age of 50; those with 25 years' experience may retire at any age.

Work Environment

Air traffic controllers are required to remain constantly alert and focused while performing a large number of simultaneous duties. They must keep track of several aircraft approaching, departing, and passing through the airspace under their control, while receiving flight data from and giving instructions to several pilots at once. They must remain alert to changes in weather and airport conditions, guide planes through intricate approach patterns, and maintain a safe separation of aircraft in the sky and on the ground. They must be able to interpret the symbols on the radar screen, form a clear image of what is happening in the sky above them, and react quickly and decisively to the activity of the aircraft. Controllers must also have strong communicative abilities and be able to give instructions to pilots in a firm and clear tone. The stress of the controller's job requires a great deal of emotional control, especially in times of potential danger and emergency. Traffic conditions change continuously throughout the controller's shift, and the controller must remain alert during times of light traffic as well as times of heavy traffic.

Terminal air traffic controllers work in towers as high as 200 feet off the ground; windows on all sides of the tower allow the pilot to see what is happening on the runways and in the sky around the airport. Radar control screens provide locations of all aircraft in the airport's airspace. Large air traffic control towers generally house the radar control center in a room below the observation tower. En route centers are usually housed in large, windowless buildings. These controllers monitor the sky entirely through radar and radio communication. Flight service stations are often located at airports in separate buildings from the control tower.

The numbers of air traffic controllers on duty varies from airport to airport and according to the number of scheduled flights expected in a center's airspace. At a small airport, a controller may work alone for an entire shift; larger airports may have up to 30 controllers on duty, while en route centers may have 150 to 700 controllers on duty during a shift. Air traffic controllers work a five-day, 40-hour week, usually on a rotating shift basis, which means they often work at night, during the week, and during holidays. Overtime is often available; during a shift, controllers are given breaks every two hours.

Outlook

Competition for air traffic control positions is high and is expected to remain high. The FAA is currently not hiring air traffic controllers, and many more qualified applicants are always attracted to the job than the number of positions available.

As more and more planes have been equipped with GPS technology, the role of the air traffic controller has come under threat. GPS allows planes to form a far more accurate picture of their position and the position of others in the sky. This allows planes to break away from the traditional air routes and essentially chart their own course, allowing for faster and more economical flights. Under pressure from the airlines, the FAA announced its intentions to adopt a "Free Flight" program, allowing the airlines to take advantage of their GPS equipment. This will mean a far more limited role for the air traffic controller, and especially en route controllers, who may see their functions reduced to monitoring aircraft and stepping in to assist in emergencies. Air traffic controllers will still be needed at the airports, although in fewer numbers. Openings in the field will come primarily from retiring controllers and others who leave the job.

For More Information

Contact the following associations for additional information on air traffic control careers:

Air Traffic Control Association
2300 Clarendon Boulevard, Suite 711
Arlington, VA 22201
Tel: 703-522-5717

Federal Aviation Administration
Office of Personnel and Training
800 Independence Avenue, SW
Washington, DC 20591
Tel: 202-366-4000

National Association of Air Traffic Specialists
4740 Corridor Place, #C
Beltsville, MD 20705
Tel: 301-933-6228

Canadian Air Traffic Control Association
162 Cleopatra Drive
Nepean, ON K26 5X2 Canada
Tel: 613-225-3553

Airplane Dispatchers

School Subjects

Geography
Mathematics

Personal Skills

Communication/ideas
Technical/scientific

Work Environment

Primarily indoors
One location with some travel

Minimum Education Level

Some postsecondary training

Salary Range

$23,000 to $47,000 to $66,000

Certification or Licensing

Required by all states

Outlook

Little change or more slowly than the average

Overview

Airplane dispatchers plan and direct commercial air flights according to government and airline company regulations. They read radio reports from airplane pilots during flights and study weather reports to determine any necessary change in flight direction or altitude. They send instructions by radio to the pilots in the case of heavy storms, fog, mechanical difficulties, or other emergencies. Airline dispatchers are sometimes called flight superintendents.

History

Commercial air service took off slowly in the United States. The first airmail flight occurred in 1911. The first passenger air service was organized in 1914, providing air transportation from Tampa to St. Petersburg, Florida, but this service lasted only six months. In 1917, however, the U.S. Post Office began its first airmail service. In 1925, the Kelly Air Mail Act turned over the airmail routes to 12 private contractors. This formed the basis of the commercial airline industry in the United States.

The airline industry developed rapidly in the years leading up to World War II. The Air Commerce Act of 1927 introduced licensing requirements for pilots and airlines and created a network of defined airways. Improvements in airplane design had brought larger, more comfortable airplanes, and the numbers of passengers reached into the millions. By 1933, the United States boasted the busiest airports in the world.

These developments created a need for people to organize and guide the increasing numbers of flights operated by the airlines. During the early days of aviation, the airplane dispatcher served in a number of capacities, including that of station manager, meteorologist, radio operator, and even mechanic. Often pilots were pressed into service as dispatchers because of their knowledge of weather and of the needs of flight crews. As the airline industry grew, these tasks became specialized. The first federal air traffic control center was opened in 1936. In 1938, federal licensing requirements were established for the airline's own dispatchers. Soon dispatchers were located all over the country.

Since that time, the work of dispatchers has become more involved and complicated, and the airline industry has relied on them extensively to make a major contribution to the safety of commercial air travel. Advancements in technology have eased parts of the airplane dispatcher's job and have also allowed the airlines to consolidate their remote dispatch offices to a smaller number of centrally located offices.

The Job

Airplane dispatchers are employed by commercial airlines, and they maintain a constant watch on factors affecting the movement of planes during flights. Dispatchers are responsible for the safety of flights and for making certain that they are operated on an efficient, profit-making basis. The work of dispatchers, however, is not the same as that of air traffic controllers, who are employees of the federal government.

Airplane dispatchers are responsible for giving the company's clearance for each flight that takes off during their shift. Their judgments are based on data received from a number of different sources. In their efforts to make certain that each flight will end successfully, they must take into consideration current weather conditions, weather forecasts, wind speed and direction, and other information. Before flights, they must decide whether the airplane crew should report to the field or whether the airline should begin notifying passengers that their flight has been delayed or canceled. Dispatchers may also have to determine whether an alternate route should be used, either to include another stop for passengers or to avoid certain weather conditions.

Upon reporting to the field before a flight, the pilot confers with the dispatcher and determines the best route to use, the amount of fuel to be placed aboard the aircraft, the altitude at which to fly, and the approximate flying time. The pilot and the dispatcher must agree on the conditions of the flight, and both have the option of delaying or canceling flights should conditions become too hazardous to ensure a safe trip.

Dispatchers may also be responsible for maintaining records and for determining the weight and balance of the aircraft after loading. They must be certain that all intended cargo is loaded aboard each of the appropriate flights. They must also be certain that all their decisions, such as those about the cargo, are in keeping with the safety regulations of the FAA, as well as with the rules established by their own airline.

Once the planes are in the air, dispatchers keep in constant contact with the flight crews. A dispatcher may be responsible for communications with as many as 10 or 12 flights at any one time. Contact is maintained through a company-owned radio network that enables each company to keep track of all of its planes. Dispatchers keep the crews informed about the weather that they will encounter, and they record the positions and other information reported by the planes while they are en route. If an emergency occurs, dispatchers coordinate the actions taken in response to the emergency.

Following each flight, the pilot checks with the dispatcher for a debriefing. In the debriefing, the pilot brings the dispatcher up to date about the weather encountered in the air and other conditions related to the flight, so that the dispatcher will have this information available in scheduling subsequent flights.

Good judgment is an important tool of airplane dispatchers, for they must be able to make fast, workable, realistic decisions. Because of this, dispatchers often experience strains and tensions on the job, especially when many flights are in the air or when an emergency occurs.

In larger airlines, there is a certain degree of specialization among dispatchers. An assistant dispatcher may work with the chief dispatcher and have the major responsibility for just one phase of the dispatching activities, such as analyzing current weather information, while a senior dispatcher may be designated to take care of another phase, such as monitoring the operating costs of each flight.

Requirements

High School

Because some college education is required to be an airplane dispatcher, high school students interested in the career should follow a college-prep curriculum. Business administration and computer skills are vital to the job, so related courses should be taken. While in high school, you can also pursue a student pilot's license, which is a great advantage, though not a requirement.

Postsecondary Training

Airplane dispatchers are required to have at least two years of college education with studies in meteorology or air transportation. Two years of work experience in air transportation may take the place of the college requirement. Airlines prefer college graduates who have studied mathematics, physics, or meteorology.

Certification or Licensing

Airplane dispatchers must be licensed by the Federal Aviation Administration. They may prepare for the FAA licensing examination in several different ways. They may work at least one year in a dispatching office under a licensed dispatcher, complete an FAA-approved airline dispatcher's course at a specialized school or training center, or show that they have spent two of the previous three years in air traffic control work or a related job.

Candidates who meet the preliminary requirements must also pass an examination covering such subjects as civil air regulations, radio procedures, airport and airway traffic procedures, weather analysis, and air-navigation facilities. In addition to a written test, they must also pass an oral examination covering the interpretation of weather information, landing and cruising speeds of various aircraft, airline routes, navigation facilities, and operational characteristics of different types of aircraft. They must not only demonstrate their knowledge of these areas to become a licensed dispatcher, but they are also expected to maintain these skills once licensed. Various training programs, some of which may be conducted by their employers, will assist them in staying current with new developments, which are frequent in this job.

Assistant dispatchers are not always required to be licensed. Thus, it may be possible to begin work in a dispatcher's office prior to earning the dispatcher's license.

Other Requirements

Airline dispatchers need to be able to work well either by themselves or with others and to assume responsibility for their decisions. Their job requires them to think and act quickly and sensibly under the most trying conditions. They may be responsible for hundreds of lives at any one time, and a poor decision could result in tragedy.

Airline dispatchers must be at least 23 years old and in good health. Their vision must be correctable to 20/20. A good memory, the ability to remain calm under great pressure and to do many things at once, and to make decisions quickly are essential to a successful airplane dispatcher's career.

Exploring

Besides pursuing the course of study mentioned previously, there is little opportunity for an individual to explore the field of airplane dispatching directly. Part-time or summer jobs with airlines may provide interested students with a chance to observe some of the activities related to dispatching work.

Employers

Virtually all airplane dispatchers are employed by commercial airlines, both those that ship cargo and those that transport passengers.

Starting Out

The occupation is not easy to enter because of its relatively small size and the special skills required. The nature of the training is such that it is not easily put to use outside of this specific area. Few people leave this career once they are in it, so only a few positions other than those caused by death or retirement become available.

People who are able to break into the field are often promoted to assistant dispatchers' jobs from related fields. They may come from among the airline's dispatch clerks, meteorologists, radio operators, or retired pilots. Obviously, airlines prefer those people who have had a long experience in ground-flight operations work. Thus, it is probably wise to plan on starting out in one of these related fields and eventually working into a position as airplane dispatcher.

Advancement

The usual path of advancement is from dispatch clerk to assistant dispatcher to dispatcher and then, possibly, to chief flight dispatcher or flight dispatch manager or assistant manager. It is also possible to become a chief flight supervisor or superintendent of flight control.

The line of advancement varies depending upon the airline, the size of the facility where the dispatcher is located, and the positions available. At smaller facilities, there may be only two or three different promotional levels available.

Earnings

Assistant airplane dispatchers for the larger airlines average earnings between $23,000 and $36,000 annually. Licensed dispatchers earn about $47,000 per year. Flight superintendents make up to about $52,800 per year, and shift chiefs, $66,000. Airline positions generally provide health insurance and other benefits. Beginning dispatchers receive two weeks paid vacation per year; after 25 years dispatchers may receive as many as six weeks vacation each year. Most dispatchers and their families are also able to fly for free or at heavily discounted prices. Smaller airlines and air companies generally pay less, with some dispatchers earning as low as $8,000 per year. Benefits may vary widely among these companies.

Work Environment

Airplane dispatchers are normally stationed at airports near a terminal or hangar, but in facilities away from the public. Some airlines use several dispatch installations, while others use a single office. Because dispatchers make decisions involving not only thousands of people but also a great deal of money, their offices are often located close to those of management, so that they can remain in close contact.

Frequently, the offices where airplane dispatchers work are full of noise and activity, with telephones ringing, computer printers chattering, and many people talking and moving about to consult charts and other sources of information. The offices usually operate 24 hours per day, with each dispatcher working eight-hour shifts, plus an additional half-hour used in briefing the relief person.

Many lives depend on airplane dispatchers every day. This means that there is often considerable stress in their jobs. Dispatchers must constantly make rapid decisions based on their evaluation of a great deal of information. Adding to the tension is the fact that they may work in noisy, hectic surroundings and must interact with many people throughout the day. However, dispatchers can feel deep satisfaction in knowing that their job is vital to the safety and success of airline operations.

Outlook

The larger airlines employ only about one thousand dispatchers. Smaller airlines and some private firms also employ airplane dispatchers, but the number of dispatchers remains very small. An expected increase in air traffic in coming years may mean a slight increase in the number of airplane dispatchers needed. However, the centralization of dispatch offices using more advanced technology means that fewer dispatchers will be able to do more work. With improved communications equipment, a single dispatcher will be able to cover a larger area than is currently possible. Because of the relatively small size of this occupational field, its employment outlook is not particularly good.

For More Information

For career books and information about high school student membership, national forums, and job fairs, contact:

Aviation Information Resources, Inc.
1001 Riverdale Court
Atlanta, GA 30337
Tel: 800-AIR-APPS
Web: http://www.airapps.com

Civil Engineering Technicians

School Subjects
Mathematics
Physics

Personal Skills
Following instructions
Technical/scientific

Work Environment
Indoors and outdoors
Primarily multiple locations

Minimum Education Level
Associate's degree

Salary Range
$16,500 to $40,000 to $71,500

Certification or Licensing
Recommended

Outlook
Faster than the average

Overview

Civil engineering technicians help civil engineers design, plan, and build public as well as private works to meet the community's needs. They are employed in a wide range of projects, such as highways, drainage systems, water and sewage facilities, railroads, subways, airports, dams, bridges, and tunnels.

History

Engineering, both military and civil, is one of the world's oldest professions. The pyramids of ancient Egypt and the bridges, roads, and aqueducts of the Roman Empire (some of which are still in use) are examples of ancient engineering feats. It was not until the 18th century in France and England that civil engineers began to organize themselves into professional societies to exchange information or plan projects. At that time, most civil engineers were still self-taught, skilled craft workers. Thomas Telford, for instance, Britain's leading road builder and first president of the Institution of Civil Engineers, started his career as a stonemason. And John Rennie, the builder of the new London Bridge, began as a millwright's apprentice.

The first major educational programs intended for civil engineers were offered by the École Polytechnique, founded in Paris in 1794. Similar courses at the Bauakadamie, founded in Berlin in 1799, and at University College London, founded in 1826, soon followed. In the United States, the first courses in civil engineering were taught at Rensselaer Polytechnic Institute, founded in 1824.

From the beginning, civil engineers have required the help of skilled assistants to handle the many details that are part of all phases of civil engineering. Traditionally, these assistants have possessed a combination of basic knowledge and good manual skills. As construction techniques have become more sophisticated, however, there is an increased need for assistants to be technically trained in specialized fields relevant to civil engineering.

These technically trained assistants are today's civil engineering technicians. Just as separate educational programs and professional identity developed for the civil engineer in the 18th and 19th centuries, so it is for civil engineering technicians in this century. The civil engineering technician is a distinguished member of the civil engineering team.

The Job

Civil engineering technicians work in many areas. State highway departments, for example, use their services to collect data, to design and draw plans, and to supervise the construction and maintenance of roadways. Railroad and airport facilities require similar services. Cities and counties need to have transportation systems, drainage systems, and water and sewage facilities planned, built, and maintained with the help of civil engineering technicians.

Civil engineering technicians participate in all stages of the construction process. During the planning stages, they help engineers prepare lists of materials needed and estimate project costs. One of the most important technician positions at this stage is the structural engineering technician. *Structural engineering technicians* help engineers calculate the size, number, and composition of beams and columns and investigate allowable soil pressures which develop from the weight of these structures. If the pressure will cause excessive settling or some other failure, they may help design special piers, rafts, pilings, or footings to prevent structural problems.

During the planning stages, civil engineering technicians help engineers prepare drawings, maps, and charts; during the actual construction phase, construction technicians assist building contractors and site supervisors in preparing work schedules and cost estimates and in performing work inspections. One of their most important duties is to ensure that each step of construction is completed before workers arrive to begin the next stage.

Some technicians specialize in certain types of construction projects. *Highway technicians,* for example, perform surveys and cost estimates as well as plan and supervise highway construction and maintenance. *Rail and waterway technicians* survey, make specifications and cost estimates, and help plan and construct railway and waterway facilities. Assistant city engineers coordinate the planning and construction of city streets, sewers, drainage systems, refuse facilities, and other major civil projects.

Other technicians specialize in certain phases of the construction process. For example, *construction materials testing technicians* sample and run tests on rock, soil, cement, asphalt, wood, steel, concrete, and other materials. *Photogrammetric technicians* use aerial photographs to prepare maps, plans, and profiles. Party chiefs work for licensed land surveyors, survey land for boundary-line locations, and plan subdivisions and other large-area land developments.

There are other specialized positions for civil engineering technicians: *research engineering technicians* test and develop new products and equipment; *sales engineering technicians* sell building materials, construction equipment, and engineering services; and *water resources technicians* gather data, make computations and drawings for water projects, and prepare economic studies.

Requirements

High School

Students should follow the course for admission into an institution offering either a two- or four-year degree in civil engineering technology. Helpful classes include mathematics, physics, and chemistry. Because the ability to read and interpret material is very important, four years of English and language skills courses are basic requirements. Reports and letters are an essential part of the technician's work, so a firm grasp of English grammar is important. Other useful courses include mechanical drawing and shop; civil engineering technicians often make use of mechanical drawings to convey their ideas to others, and neat, well-executed drawings are important to convey a sense of accuracy and competence.

Postsecondary Training

Students should be careful to choose a school that offers an accredited program in civil engineering technology. In such programs, more mathematics and science subjects, including physics, will be studied to prepare the student for later specialty courses, such as surveying, materials, hydraulics, highway and bridge construction and design, structures, railway and water systems, heavy construction, soils, steel and concrete construction, cost and estimates, and management and construction technology. Students should also take courses in computer programming and photogrammetry.

Certification or Licensing

To advance in professional standing, civil engineering technicians should try to become Certified Engineering Technicians.

Other Requirements

Civil engineering projects are often complex and long-term, requiring a variety of specialized skills. Civil engineering technicians need the ability to think and plan ahead, as well as the patience to work through all the necessary details. "The devil is in the details" could be the motto for the engineering technicians whose job it is to see that each part of the whole project is correct.

Exploring

One of the best ways to acquire first-hand experience in this field is through part-time or summer work with a construction company. Even if the job is menial, you can still observe surveying teams, site supervisors, building inspectors, skilled craft workers, and civil engineering technicians at work. If such work is not possible, students can organize field trips to various construction sites or to facilities where building materials are manufactured.

Employers

Civil engineers work for various construction companies and, very frequently, for the government. Some choose to go into business for themselves after acquiring a great deal of experience working for others.

Starting Out

Most schools maintain placement offices, which many prospective employers contact when they have job openings. The placement offices, in turn, help the student or graduate prepare a resume of relevant school and work experiences, and usually arrange personal interviews with prospective employers. Many schools also have cooperative work-study programs with particular companies and government agencies. With such a program, the company or government agency often becomes the new technician's place of full-time employment after graduation.

Advancement

Civil engineering technicians must study and learn throughout their careers. They must learn new techniques, master the operation of new equipment, and gain greater depth of knowledge in their chosen fields to keep themselves abreast of the latest developments. Some technicians move on to supervisory positions, while others pursue additional education to become civil engineers.

Earnings

Civil engineering technicians usually begin their first jobs at a salary range of $16,500 to $29,000 a year, with the higher paying jobs going to those with advanced education. Most experienced technicians earn between $33,000 to $49,390 or more annually. Some senior technicians earn as much as $71,500 a year or more. The incomes of many civil engineering technicians who operate their own construction, surveying, or equipment businesses are excellent. Some of these companies can earn millions of dollars each year.

Paid vacations, pension plans, and insurance are normal parts of the benefits paid to civil engineering technicians. Many companies pay a bonus if a job is completed ahead of schedule or if the job is completed for less than the estimated cost. These bonuses sometimes amount to more than the employee's regular annual salary.

Work Environment

Technicians usually work 40 hours a week with extra pay for overtime. Working conditions vary from job to job: technicians who enjoy being outdoors may choose a job in construction or surveying; those who prefer working indoors may work in a consulting engineer's office on computations, drafting, or design. In either case, the work done by civil engineering technicians is usually cleaner than the work done by most other construction trades workers.

Civil engineering technicians feel the pride that comes from being a member of a team that constructs major buildings, bridges, or dams. In a way, such projects become monuments to the efforts of each member of the team. And there is the accompanying satisfaction that the project has improved, if only in a modest way, the quality of life in a community.

Outlook

The outlook for civil engineering technicians is generally favorable. As in most industries, those with certification and the most education have the best outlook. Construction is, however, one of the industries most likely to feel the effects of economic recessions, so civil engineering technicians must be prepared for slowdowns in business.

For More Information

This organization offers the brochure "Engineering: Your Future" online:

American Society for Engineering Education
11 Dupont Circle, Suite 200
Washington, DC 20036
Tel: 202-331-3500
Web: http://www.asee.org

For information on careers and scholarships, send a self-addressed, stamped envelope to the following:

American Society of Certified Engineering Technicians
PO Box 1348
Flowery Branch, GA 30542
Tel: 404-967-9173

American Society of Civil Engineers
1801 Alexander Bell Drive
Reston, VA 20191-4400
Tel: 703-295-6000
Web: http://www.asce.org

Civil Engineers

School Subjects
Mathematics
Physics

Personal Skills
Leadership/management
Technical/scientific

Work Environment
Indoors and outdoors
Primarily multiple locations

Minimum Education Level
Bachelor's degree

Salary Range
$33,000 to $46,000 to $117,000

Certification or Licensing
Required by all states

Outlook
Faster than the average

Overview

Civil engineers are involved in the design and construction of the physical structures that make up our surroundings, such as roads, bridges, buildings, and harbors. Civil engineering involves theoretical knowledge applied to the practical planning of the layout of our cities, towns, and other communities. It is concerned with modifying the natural environment and building new environments to better the lifestyles of the general public. Civil engineers are also known as *structural engineers*.

History

One might trace the evolution of civil engineering methods by considering the building and many reconstructions of England's London Bridge. In Roman and medieval times, several bridges made of timber were built over the Thames River. Around the end of the 12th century, these were rebuilt into 19 narrow arches mounted on piers. A chapel was built on one of the piers, and two towers were built for defense. A fire damaged the bridge around 1212, yet the surrounding area was considered a preferred place to live and work, largely because it was the only bridge over which one could cross the river. The structure was rebuilt many times during later centuries using different materials and designs. By 1830, it had only five arches. More than a century later, the center span of the bridge was remodeled, and part of it was actually transported to the United States to be set up as a tourist attraction.

Working materials for civil engineers have changed during many centuries. For instance, bridges, once made of timber, then of iron and steel, are today made mainly with concrete that is reinforced with steel. The high strength of the material is necessary because of the abundance of cars and other heavy vehicles that travel over the bridges.

As the population continues to grow and communities become more complex, structures that civil engineers must pay attention to have to be remodeled and repaired. New highways, buildings, airstrips, and so forth must be designed to accommodate public needs. Today, more and more civil engineers are involved with water treatment plants, water purification plants, and toxic waste sites. Increasing concern about the natural environment is also evident in the growing number of engineers working on such projects as preservation of wetlands, maintenance of national forests, and restoration of sites around land mines, oil wells, and industrial factories.

The Job

Civil engineers use their knowledge of materials science, engineering theory, economics, and demographics to devise, construct, and maintain our physical surroundings. They apply their understanding of other branches of science—such as hydraulics, geology, and physics—to design the optimal blueprint for the project.

Feasibility studies are conducted by *surveying and mapping engineers* to determine the best sites and approaches for construction. They extensively investigate the chosen sites to verify that the ground and other surroundings are amenable to the proposed project. These engineers use sophisticated equipment, such as satellites and other electronic instruments, to measure the area and conduct underground probes for bedrock and groundwater. They determine the optimal places where explosives should be blasted in order to cut through rock.

Many civil engineers work strictly as consultants on projects, advising their clients. These consultants usually specialize in one area of the industry, such as water systems, transportation systems, or housing structures. Clients include individuals, corporations, and the government. Consultants will devise an overall design for the proposed project, perhaps a nuclear power plant commissioned by an electric company. They will estimate the cost of constructing the plant, supervise the feasibility studies and site investigations, and advise the client on whom to hire for the actual labor involved. Consultants are also responsible for such details as accuracy of drawings and quantities of materials to order.

Other civil engineers work mainly as contractors and are responsible for the actual building of the structure; they are known as construction engineers. They interpret the consultants' designs and follow through with the best methods for getting the work done, usually working directly at the construction site. Contractors are responsible for scheduling the work, buying the materials, maintaining surveys of the progress of the work, and choosing the machines and other equipment used for construction. During construction, these civil engineers must supervise the labor and make sure the work is completed correctly and efficiently. After the project is finished, they must set up a maintenance schedule and periodically check the structure for a certain length of time. Later, the task of ongoing maintenance and repair is often transferred to local engineers.

Civil engineers may be known by their area of specialization. *Transportation engineers,* for example, are concerned mainly with the construction of highways and mass transit systems, such as subways and commuter rail lines. When devising plans for subways, engineers are responsible for considering the tunneling that is involved. *Pipeline engineers* are specialized civil engineers who are involved with the movement of water, oil, and gas through miles of pipeline.

Requirements

High School

Because a bachelor's degree is considered essential in the field, high school students interested in civil engineering must follow a college prep curriculum. Students should focus on mathematics (algebra, trigonometry, geometry, and calculus), the sciences (physics and chemistry), computer science, and English and the humanities (history, economics, and sociology). Students should also aim for honors-level courses.

Postsecondary Training

In addition to completing the core engineering curriculum (including mathematics, science, drafting, and computer applications), students can choose their specialty from the following types of courses: structural analysis; materials design and specification; geology; hydraulics; surveying and design graphics; soil mechanics; and oceanography. Bachelor's degrees can be achieved through a number of programs: a four- or five-year accredited college or university; two years in a community college engineering program plus two or three years in a college or university; or five or six years in a co-op program (attending classes for part of the year and working in an engineering-related job for the rest of the year). About 30 percent of civil engineering students go on to receive a master's degree.

Certification or Licensing

Most civil engineers go on to study and qualify for a professional engineer (P.E.) license. It is required before one can work on projects affecting property, health, or life. Because many engineering jobs are found in government specialties, most engineers take the necessary steps to obtain the license. Registration guidelines are different for each state—they involve educational, practical, and teaching experience. Applicants must take an examination on a specified date.

Other Requirements

Basic personal characteristics often found in civil engineers are an avid curiosity; a passion for mathematics and science; an aptitude for problem solving, both alone and with a team; and an ability to visualize multidimensional, spatial relationships.

Exploring

High school students can become involved in civil engineering by attending a summer camp or study program in the field. For example, the Worcester Polytechnic Institute in Massachusetts has a 12-day summer program for students in junior and senior high school. Studies and events focus on science and math and include specialties for those interested in civil engineering.

After high school, another way to learn about civil engineering duties is to work on a construction crew that is involved in the actual building of a project designed and supervised by engineers. Such hands-on experience would provide an opportunity to work near many types of civil workers. Try to work on highway crews or even in housing construction.

Starting Out

To establish a career as a civil engineer, one must first receive a bachelor's degree in engineering or another appropriate scientific field. College placement offices are often the best sources of employment for beginning engineers. Entry-level jobs usually involve routine work, often as a member of a supervised team. After a year or more (depending on job performance and qualifications), one becomes a junior engineer, then an assistant to perhaps one or more supervising engineers. Establishment as a professional engineer comes after passing the P.E. exam.

Advancement

Professional engineers with many years' experience often join with partners to establish their own firms in design, consulting, or contracting. Some leave long-held positions to be assigned as top executives in industries such as manufacturing and business consulting. Also, there are those who return to academia to teach high school or college students. For all of these potential opportunities, it is necessary to keep abreast of engineering advancements and trends by reading industry journals and taking courses.

Earnings

Civil engineers are among the lowest paid in the engineering field. However, starting salaries are usually higher than for other occupations. Entry-level civil engineers with a bachelor's degree earn approximately $33,000 per year in private industry; those with a master's degree, about $35,000; and those with a doctorate, about $47,000. Those working in government jobs earn less than civil engineers at private companies. As with all occupations, salaries are higher for those with more experience. The average salary for those in mid-level positions is $46,000 in private industry and $61,000 in government jobs. Top civil engineers earn as much as $100,000 a year.

Work Environment

Many civil engineers work regular 40-hour weeks, often in or near major industrial and commercial areas. Sometimes they are assigned to work in remote areas and foreign countries. Because of the diversity of civil engineering positions, working conditions vary widely. Offices, labs, factories, and actual sites are typical environments for engineers. About 40 percent of all civil engineers can be found working for various levels of government, usually involving large public-works projects, such as highways and bridges.

A typical work cycle involving various types of civil engineers involves three stages: planning, constructing, and maintaining. Those involved with development of a campus compound, for example, would first need to work in their offices developing plans for a survey. Surveying and mapping engineers would have to visit the proposed site to take measurements and perhaps shoot aerial photographs. The measurements and photos would have to be converted into drawings and blueprints. Geotechnical engineers would dig wells at the site and take core samples from the ground. If toxic waste or unexpected water is found at the site, the contractor determines what should be done.

Actual construction then begins. Very often, a field trailer on the site becomes the engineers' makeshift offices. The campus might take several years to build—it is not uncommon for engineers to be involved in long-term projects. If contractors anticipate that deadlines will not be met, they often put in weeks of 10- to 15-hour days on the job.

After construction is complete, engineers spend less and less time at the site. Some may be assigned to stay on-site to keep daily surveys of how the structure is holding up and to solve problems when they arise. Eventually, the project engineers finish the job and move on to another long-term assignment.

Outlook

Through the year 2006, civil engineers are expected to experience steady employment for the maintenance and repair of public works, such as highways and water systems. The need for civil engineers will depend somewhat on the government's decisions to spend further on renewing and adding to the country's basic infrastructure. As public awareness of environmental issues continues to increase, civil engineers will find expanding employment opportunities at wastewater sites, recycling establishments, and toxic dump sites for industrial and municipal waste.

For More Information

For information on careers and scholarships, contact:

American Society of Civil Engineers
1801 Alexander Bell Drive
Reston, VA 20191-4400
Tel: 703-295-6000
Web: http://www.asce.org

For information on careers, scholarships, and a list of accredited schools, contact:

Institute of Transportation Engineers
525 School Street, SW, Suite 410
Washington, DC 20024
Tel: 202-554-8050
Web: http://www.ite.org

For information on careers in engineering, contact:

Junior Engineering Technical Society, Inc.
1420 King Street, Suite 405
Alexandria, VA 22314
Tel: 703-548-5387
Web: http://www.asee.org/external/jets

For information on their 12-day summer engineering program for students in junior and senior high school, contact:

Worcester Polytechnic Institute
Frontiers in Science, Mathematics, and Engineering
100 Institute Road
Worcester, MA 01609
Tel: 508-831-5000
Web: http://cs.wpi.edu

Customs Officials

School Subjects
English
Government

Personal Skills
Communication/ideas
Helping/teaching

Work Environment
Primarily indoors
Primarily one location

Minimum Education Level
High school diploma

Salary Range
$20,588 to $31,195 to $45,235

Certification or Licensing
None available

Outlook
Faster than the average

Overview

Customs officials are federal workers who are employed by the United States Customs Service (an arm of the Treasury Department) to enforce laws governing imports and exports and to combat smuggling and revenue fraud. The U.S. Customs Service generates revenue for the government by assessing and collecting duties and excise taxes on imported merchandise. Amid a whirl of international travel and commercial activity, customs officials process travelers, baggage, cargo, and mail, as well as administer certain navigation laws. Stationed in the United States and overseas at airports, seaports, and all crossings, as well as at points along the Canadian and Mexican borders, customs officials examine, count, weigh, gauge, measure, and sample commercial and noncommercial cargoes entering and leaving the United States. It is their job to determine whether or not goods are admissible and, if so, how much tax, or duty, should be assessed on them. To prevent smuggling, fraud, and cargo theft, customs officials also check the individual baggage declarations of international travelers and oversee the unloading of all types of commercial shipments.

History

Countries collect taxes on imports and sometimes on exports as a means of producing revenue for the government. Export duties were first introduced in England in the year 1275 by a statute that levied taxes on animal hides and on wool. American colonists in the 1700s objected to the import duties England forced them to pay (levied under the Townshend Acts), charging "taxation without representation." Although the British government rescinded the Townshend Acts, it retained the tax on tea, which led to the Boston Tea Party on December 16, 1773.

After the American Revolution, delegates at the Constitutional Convention decided that "no tax or duty shall be laid on articles exported from any state," but they approved taxing imports from abroad. The customs service was established by the First Congress in 1789 as part of the Treasury Department. Until 1816 these customs assessments were used primarily for revenue. The Tariff Act of 1816 declared, however, that the main function of customs laws was to protect American industry from foreign companies. By 1927 the customs service was established as a separate bureau within the Treasury Department. Today, the U.S. Customs Service oversees more than 400 laws and regulations, including those from 40 different government agencies, generating more government money than any other federal agency besides the Internal Revenue Service (IRS).

The Job

Like shrewd detectives, customs officials enforce U.S. Customs Service laws by controlling imports and exports and by combating smuggling and revenue frauds. They make sure that people, ships, planes, and trains—anything used to import or export cargo—comply with all entrance and clearance requirements at borders and ports.

Customs inspectors carefully and thoroughly examine cargo to make sure that it matches the description on a ship's or aircraft's manifest. They inspect baggage and personal items worn or carried by travelers entering or leaving the United States by ship, plane, or automobile. Inspectors are authorized to go aboard a ship or plane to determine the exact nature of the cargo being transported. In the course of a single day they review cargo manifests, inspect cargo containers, and supervise unloading activities to prevent smuggling, fraud, or cargo thefts. They may have to weigh and measure imports to see that commerce laws are being followed and to protect American distributors in cases where restricted trademarked merchandise is being brought into the country. In this way, they can protect the interests of American companies.

Customs inspectors examine crew and passenger lists, sometimes in cooperation with the police, who may be searching for criminals. They are authorized to search suspicious individuals and to arrest them if necessary. They are also allowed to conduct body searches of suspected individuals to check for contraband. They check health clearances and ship's documents in an effort to prevent the spread of disease that may require quarantine.

Individual baggage declarations of international travelers also come under their scrutiny. Inspectors who have baggage examination duty at points of entry into the United States classify purchases made abroad and, if necessary, assess and collect duties. All international travelers are allowed to bring home certain quantities of foreign purchases, such as perfume, clothing, tobacco, and liquor, without paying taxes. However, they must declare the amount and value of their purchases on a customs form. If they have made purchases above the duty-free limits, they must pay taxes. Customs inspectors are prepared to advise tourists about U.S. Customs regulations and allow them to change their customs declarations if necessary and pay the duty before baggage inspection. Inspectors must be alert and observant to detect undeclared items. If any are discovered, it is up to the inspector to decide whether an oversight or deliberate fraud has occurred. Sometimes the contraband is held and a U.S. Customs hearing is scheduled to decide the case. A person who is caught trying to avoid paying duty is fined. When customs violations occur, inspectors must file detailed reports and often later appear as witnesses in court.

Customs officials often work with other government agents and are sometimes required to be armed. They cooperate with special agents for the Federal Bureau of Investigation (FBI), the Drug Enforcement Administration (DEA), the U.S. Immigration and Naturalization Service (INS), the Food and Drug Administration (FDA), and public health officials and agricultural quarantine inspectors.

Business magnates, ships' captains, and importers are among those with whom customs inspectors have daily contact as they review manifests, examine cargo, and control shipments transferred under bond to ports throughout the United States.

Some of the specialized fields for customs officials are as follows:

Customs patrol officers conduct surveillance at points of entry into the United States to prohibit smuggling and detect customs violations. They try to catch people illegally transporting smuggled merchandise and contraband such as narcotics, watches, jewelry, and weapons, as well as fruits, plants, and meat that may be infested with pests or diseases. Armed and equipped with two-way communication devices, they function much like police officers. On the waterfront, customs patrol officers monitor piers, ships, and crew members and are constantly on the lookout for items being thrown from the ship to small boats nearby. Customs patrol officers provide security at entrance and exit facilities of piers and airports, make sure all baggage is checked, and maintain security at loading, exit, and entrance areas of customs buildings and during the transfer of legal drug shipments to prevent hijackings or theft.

Using informers and other sources, they gather intelligence information about illegal activities. When probable cause exists, they are authorized to take possible violators into custody, using physical force or weapons if necessary. They assist other customs personnel in developing or testing new enforcement techniques and equipment.

Customs pilots, who must have a current Federal Aviation Administration (FAA) commercial pilot's license, conduct air surveillance of illegal traffic crossing U.S. borders by air, land, or sea. They apprehend, arrest, and search violators and prepare reports used to prosecute the criminals. They are stationed along the Canadian and Mexican borders as well as along coastal areas, flying single- and multiengine planes and helicopters.

Canine enforcement officers train and use dogs to prevent smuggling of all controlled substances as defined by customs laws. These controlled substances include marijuana, narcotics, and dangerous drugs. After undergoing an intensive 15-week basic training course in the Detector Dog Training Center, where each officer is paired with a dog and assigned to a post, canine enforcement officers work in cooperation with customs inspectors, customs patrol officers, and special agents to find and seize contraband and arrest smugglers. Currently, most canine enforcement officers are used at entry points along the border with Mexico.

Import specialists become technical experts in a particular line of merchandise, such as wine or electronic equipment. They keep up-to-date on their area of specialization by going to trade shows and importers' places of business. Merchandise for delivery to commercial importers is examined, classified, and appraised by these specialists, who must enforce import quotas and trademark laws. They use import quotas and current market values to determine the unit value of the merchandise in order to calculate the amount of money due the government in tariffs. Import specialists routinely question importers, check their lists, and make sure the merchandise matches the description and the list. If they find a violation, they call for a formal inquiry by customs special agents. Import specialists regularly deal with problems of fraud and violations of copyright and trademark laws. If the importer meets federal requirements, the import specialist issues a permit that authorizes the release of merchandise for delivery. If not, the goods might be seized and sold at public auction. These specialists encourage international trade by authorizing the lowest allowable duties on merchandise.

Customs service chemists form a subgroup of import specialists who protect the health and safety of Americans. They analyze imported merchandise for textile fibers, lead content, and narcotics. In many cases, the duty collected on imported products depends on the chemist's analysis and subsequent report. Customs chemists often serve as expert witnesses in court. The customs laboratories in Boston; New York; Baltimore; Savannah; New Orleans; Los Angeles; San Francisco; Chicago; Washington, DC; and San Juan, Puerto Rico, have specialized instruments that can analyze materials for their chemical components. These machines can determine such things as the amount of sucrose in a beverage, the fiber content of a textile product, the lead oxide content of fine crystal, or the presence of toxic chemicals and prohibited additives.

Criminal investigators, or *special agents,* are plainclothes investigators who make sure that the government obtains revenue on imports and that contraband and controlled substances do not enter or leave the country illegally. They investigate smuggling, criminal fraud, and major cargo thefts. Special agents target professional criminals as well as ordinary tourists who give false information on baggage declarations. Often working undercover, they cooperate with customs inspectors and the FBI. Allowed special powers of entry, search, seizure, and arrest, special agents have the broadest powers of search of any law enforcement personnel in the United States. For instance, special agents do not need probable cause or a warrant to justify search or seizure near a border or port of entry. However, in the interior of the United States, probable cause but not a warrant is necessary to conduct a search.

Requirements

High School

If you are interested in working for the U.S. Customs Service, you should pursue a well-rounded education in high school. Courses in government, geography and social studies, English, and history will contribute to your understanding of international and domestic legal issues as well as giving you a good general background. If you wish to become a specialist in scientific or investigative aspects of the Customs Service, courses in the sciences, particularly chemistry, will be necessary and courses in computer science will be helpful.

Postsecondary Training

Applicants to the U.S. Customs Service must be U.S. citizens and at least 21 years of age. They must have earned at least a high school diploma, but applicants with college degrees are preferred. Applicants are required to have three years of general work experience involving contact with the public or four years of college.

Like all federal employees, applicants to the U.S. Customs Service must pass a physical examination and undergo a security check. They must also pass a federally administered standardized test, called the Professional and Administrative Career Examination (PACE). Entrance-level appointments are at grades GS-5 and GS-7, depending on the level of education or work experience.

Special agents must establish an eligible rating on the Treasury Enforcement Examination (TEE), a test that measures investigative aptitude; successfully complete an oral interview; pass a personal background investigation; and be in excellent physical condition. Although they receive extensive training, these agents need to have two years of specialized criminal investigative or comparable experience. Applicants with the necessary specialized law-enforcement experience or education should establish eligibility on the Mid-Level Register for appointment grades GS-9, 11, and 12.

Other Requirements

Applicants must be in good physical condition, possess emotional and mental stability, and demonstrate the ability to correctly apply regulations or instructional material and make clear, concise oral or written reports.

Exploring

There are several ways for you to learn about the various positions available at the U.S. Customs Service. You can talk with people employed as customs inspectors, consult your high school counselors, or contact local labor union organizations and offices for additional information. Information on federal government jobs is available from offices of the state employment service, area offices of the U.S. Office of Personnel Management, and Federal Job Information Centers throughout the country.

Employers

The U.S. Customs Service is the sole employer of customs officials.

Starting Out

Applicants may enter the various occupations of the U.S. Customs Service by applying to take the appropriate civil service examinations. Interested applicants should note the age, citizenship, and experience requirements previously described and realize that they will undergo a background check and a drug test. If hired, applicants will receive exacting, on-the-job training.

Advancement

All customs agents have the opportunity to advance through a special system of promotion from within. Although they enter at the GS-5 or GS-7 level, after one year they may compete for promotion to supervisory positions or simply to positions at a higher grade level in the agency. The journeyman level is grade GS-9. Supervisory positions at GS-11 and above are available on a competitive basis. After attaining permanent status (i.e., serving for one year on probation), customs patrol officers may compete to become special agents. Entry-level appointments for customs chemists are made at GS-5. However, applicants with advanced degrees or professional experience in the sciences, or both, should qualify for higher-graded positions. Advancement potential exists for the journeyman level at GS-11 and to specialist, supervisory, and management positions at grades GS-12 and above.

Earnings

The federal government employs approximately 75,000 customs workers. Entry-level positions at GS-5 paid $20,588 in 1999, and entry at GS-7 paid $25,501 per year. The average GS ranking among customs officials was 9.3, which correlates to an annual salary of over $31,195. Supervisory positions beginning at GS-11 and GS-12 paid $37,744 and $45,236, respectively. Federal employees in certain cities receive locality pay in addition to their salaries in order to offset the higher cost of living in those areas. Locality pay generally adds an extra 5.6 to 12 percent to the base salary. Certain customs officials are also entitled to receive Law Enforcement Availability Pay, which adds another 25 percent to their salaries. All federal workers receive annual cost-of-living salary increases. Federal workers enjoy generous benefits, including health and life insurance, pension plans, and holiday, sick leave, and vacation pay.

Work Environment

The customs territory of the United States is divided into nine regions that include the 50 states, the District of Columbia, Puerto Rico, and the U.S. Virgin Islands. In these regions there are some 300 ports of entry along land and sea borders. Customs inspectors may be assigned to any of these ports or to overseas work at airports, seaports, waterfronts, border stations, customs houses, or the U.S. Customs Service Headquarters in Washington, DC. They are able to request assignments in certain localities and usually receive them when possible.

A typical work schedule is eight hours a day, five days a week, but customs employees often work overtime or long into the night. United States entry and exit points must be supervised 24 hours a day, which means that workers rotate night shifts and weekend duty. Customs inspectors and patrol officers are sometimes assigned to one-person border points at remote locations, where they may perform immigration and agricultural inspections in addition to regular duties. They often risk physical injury from criminals violating customs regulations.

Outlook

Employment as a customs official is steady work that is not affected by changes in the economy. With the increased emphasis on law enforcement, including the detection of illegally imported drugs and pornography and the prevention of exports of sensitive high-technology items, the prospects for steady employment in the U.S. Customs Service are likely to grow and remain high.

For More Information

For career and employment information, contact:

U.S. Customs Service
Office of Human Resources
1300 Pennsylvania Avenue, NW
Washington, DC 20229
Tel: 202-927-2900
Web: http://www.customs.ustreas.gov

Diesel Mechanics

School Subjects

Computer science
Technical/Shop

Personal Skills

Following instructions
Mechanical/manipulative

Work Environment

Primarily indoors
Primarily one location

Minimum Education Level

High school diploma

Salary Range

$20,000 to $32,000 to $40,000

Certification or Licensing

Recommended

Outlook

About as fast as the average

Overview

Diesel mechanics repair and maintain diesel engines that power trucks, buses, ships, construction and roadbuilding equipment, farm equipment, and some automobiles. They may also maintain and repair nonengine components, such as brakes, electrical systems, and heating and air conditioning.

History

In 1892, Rudolf Diesel patented an engine that despite its weight and large size was more efficient than the gasoline engine patented by Gottlieb Daimler less than a decade earlier. While Daimler's engine became the standard for automobiles, Diesel found his engine had practical use for industry. The diesel engine differs from the gasoline engine in that the ignition of fuel is caused by compression of air in the engine's cylinders rather than by a spark. Diesel's engines were eventually used to power pipelines, electric and water plants, automobiles and trucks, and marine craft. Equipment used in mines, oil fields, factories, and transoceanic shipping also came to rely on diesel engines. With the onset of World War I, diesel engines became standard in submarines, tanks, and other heavy equipment. Suddenly, diesel mechanics were in big demand and the armed forces established training programs. Combat units supported by diesel-powered machines often had several men trained in diesel mechanics to repair breakdowns. The war proved to industry that diesel engines were tough and efficient, and many companies found applications for diesel-powered machines in the following years.

At the turn of the century, trucks were wooden wagons equipped with gasoline engines. As they became bigger, transported more goods, and traveled farther, fuel efficiency became a big concern. In 1930, the trucking industry adopted the diesel engine, with its efficiency and durability, as its engine for the future. Many diesel mechanics began their training as automobile mechanics, and learned diesel through hands-on experience. World War II brought a new demand for highly trained diesel mechanics, and again the armed forces trained men in diesel technology. After the war, diesel mechanics found new jobs in diesel at trucking companies that maintained large fleets of trucks, and at construction companies that used diesel powered equipment. It wasn't until the 1970s that diesel engines in consumer passenger cars began to gain popularity. Before then, the disadvantages of diesel—its heaviness, poor performance, and low driving comfort—made diesel a second choice for many consumers. But the fuel crisis of the 1970s brought diesel a greater share of the automotive market, creating more demand for mechanics who could repair and maintain diesel engines.

Today, job growth and security for diesel mechanics is closely tied to the trucking industry. In the 1980s and 1990s, the trucking industry experienced steady growth as other means of transportation, such as rail, were used less frequently. Now, many businesses and manufacturers have found it cost efficient to maintain less inventory. Instead, they prefer to have their materials shipped on an as-needed basis. This low-inventory system has created a tremendous demand on the trucking industry, and diesel mechanics are essential to helping the industry meet that demand.

The Job

Most diesel mechanics work on the engines of heavy trucks, such as those used in hauling freight over long distances, or in heavy industries such as construction and mining. Many are employed by companies that maintain their own fleet of vehicles. The diesel mechanic's main task is preventive maintenance to avoid breakdowns, but they also make engine repairs when necessary. Diesel mechanics also frequently perform maintenance on other nonengine components, such as brake systems, electronics, transmissions, and suspensions.

Through periodic maintenance, diesel mechanics keep vehicles or engines in good operating condition. They run through a checklist of standard maintenance tasks, such as changing oil and filters, checking cooling systems, and inspecting brakes and wheel bearings for wear. They make the appropriate repairs or adjustments and replace parts that are worn. Fuel injection units, fuel pumps, pistons, crankshafts, bushings, and bearings must be regularly removed, reconditioned, or replaced.

As more diesel engines rely on a variety of electronic components, mechanics have become more proficient in the basics of electronics. Previously technical functions in diesel equipment (both engine and nonengine parts) are being replaced by electronics, significantly altering the way mechanics perform maintenance and repairs. As new technology evolves, diesel mechanics may need additional training to use tools and computers to diagnose and correct problems with electronic parts. Employers generally provide this training.

Diesel engines are scheduled for periodic rebuilding usually every 18 months or 100,000 miles. Mechanics rely upon extensive records they keep on each engine to determine the extent of the rebuild. Records detail the maintenance and repair history that helps mechanics determine repair needs and prevent future breakdowns. Diesel mechanics use various specialty instruments to make precision measurements and diagnostics of each engine component. Micrometers and various gauges test for engine wear. Ohmmeters, ammeters, and voltmeters test electrical components. Dynamometers and oscilloscopes test overall engine operations.

Engine rebuilds usually require several mechanics, each specializing in a particular area. They use ordinary hand tools such as ratchets and sockets, screwdrivers, wrenches, and pliers; power tools such as pneumatic wrenches; welding and flame-cutting equipment; and machine tools like lathes and boring machines. Diesel mechanics supply their own hand tools at an investment of $6,000 to $25,000, depending upon their specialty. It is the employer's responsibility to furnish the larger power tools, engine analyzers, and other diagnostic equipment.

In addition to trucks and buses, diesel mechanics also service and repair construction equipment such as cranes, bulldozers, earth moving equipment, and road construction equipment. The variations in transmissions, gear systems, electronics, and other engine components of diesel engines may require additional training.

To maintain and increase their skills and to keep up with new technology, diesel mechanics must regularly read service and repair manuals, industry bulletins, and other publications. They must also be willing to take part in training programs given by manufacturers or at vocational schools. Those who have certification must periodically retake exams to keep their credentials. Frequent changes in technology demand that mechanics keep up-to-date with the latest training.

Requirements

High School

A high school diploma is the minimum requirement to land a job that offers growth possibilities, a good salary, and challenges. In addition to automotive and shop classes, high school students should take mathematics, English, and computer classes. Adjustments and repairs to many car components require the mechanic to make numerous computations, for which good mathematical skills will be essential. Diesel mechanics must be voracious readers in order to stay competitive; there are many must-read volumes of repair manuals and trade journals. Computer skills are also important as computers are common in most repair shops.

Postsecondary Training

Employers prefer to hire those who have completed some kind of formal training program in diesel mechanics, or in some cases automobile mechanics—usually a minimum of two years' education in either case. A wide variety of such programs are offered at community colleges, vocational schools, independent organizations, and manufacturers. Most accredited programs include periods of internship.

Some programs are conducted in association with truck and heavy equipment manufacturers. Students combine work experience with hands-on classroom study of up-to-date equipment provided by manufacturers. In other programs students alternate time in the classroom with internships at manufacturers. Although these students may take up to four years to finish their training, they become familiar with the latest technology and also earn modest salaries as they train.

Certification or Licensing

One indicator of quality for entry-level mechanics recognized by everyone in the industry is certification by the National Automotive Technicians Education Foundation. NATEF offers certification through many secondary and postsecondary training programs throughout the country. Enrolling in a certified program assures students that the program meets the standards employers expect from their entry-level employees.

Other Requirements

Diesel mechanics must be patient and thorough in their work. They require excellent troubleshooting skills and must be able to logically deduce the cause of system malfunctions. Diesel mechanics also need a Class A driver's license.

Exploring

Many community centers offer general auto maintenance workshops where students can get additional practice working on real cars and learn from instructors. Trade magazines such as *Landline* and *Overdrive* are an excellent source for learning what's new in the trucking industry and can be found at libraries and some larger bookstores. Working part-time at a repair shop or dealership can prepare students for the atmosphere and challenges a mechanic faces on the job.

Many diesel mechanics begin their exploration on gasoline engines because spare diesel engines are hard to come by for those who are just trying to learn and experiment. Diesel engines are very similar to gasoline engines except for their ignition systems and size. Besides being larger, diesel engines are distinguished by the absence of common gasoline engine components such as spark plugs, ignition wires, coils, and distributors. Diesel mechanics use the same hand tools as automobile mechanics, however, and in this way learning technical aptitude on automobiles will be important for the student who wishes to eventually learn to work on diesel engines.

Employers

Diesel mechanics may find employment in a number of different areas. Many work for dealers that sell semi trucks and other diesel powered equipment. About 20 percent of the 266,000 diesel mechanics employed in 1996 worked for local and long distance trucking companies. Other mechanics maintain the buses and trucks of public transit companies, schools, or governments. Diesel mechanics can find work all over the country, in both large and small cities. Job titles may range from bus maintenance technician to hydraulic system technician, clutch rebuilder, and heavy duty maintenance mechanic. A small number of diesel mechanics may find jobs in the railway and industrial sectors and in marine maintenance.

Starting Out

The best way to begin a career as a diesel mechanic is to enroll in a postsecondary training program and obtain accreditation. Trade and technical schools nearly always provide job placement assistance for their graduates. Such schools usually have contacts with local employers who need to hire well-trained people. Often, employers post job openings at accredited trade schools in their area.

Although postsecondary training programs are more widely available and popular today, some mechanics still learn the trade on the job as apprentices. Their training consists of working for several years under the guidance of experienced mechanics. Trainees usually begin as helpers, lubrication workers, or service station attendants, and gradually acquire the skills and knowledge necessary for many service or repair tasks. However, fewer employers today are willing to hire apprentices because of the time and cost it takes to train them. Those who do learn their skills on the job inevitably require some formal training if they wish to advance and stay in step with the changing industry. Despite employers' preference to hire trained, accredited workers, demand is expected to exceed the number of postsecondary graduates through the year 2006, thus keeping apprentice options open for the near future. An apprenticeship is an excellent way to gain hands-on experience.

Intern programs sponsored by truck manufacturers or independent organizations provide students with opportunities to actually work with prospective employers. Internships can provide students with valuable contacts who will be able to recommend future employers once students have completed their classroom training. Many students may even be hired by the company for which they interned.

Advancement

Like NATEF training programs, currently employed mechanics may be certified by the National Institute for Automotive Service Excellence (ASE) in medium and heavy truck repair. Certification is available in gasoline engines, diesel engines, drive train, brakes, suspension and steering, preventive maintenance inspection, and electrical systems. Although certification is voluntary, it is a widely recognized standard of achievement for diesel mechanics and the way many advance. The more certification a mechanic has, the more his or her worth to an employer, and the higher he or she advances. Those who pass all seven exams earn the status of master truck mechanic. To maintain their certification, mechanics must retake the examination for their specialties every five years. Some employers will only hire NATEF-accredited mechanics and base starting salary on the level of the mechanic's accreditation.

With today's complex diesel engine and truck components requiring hundreds of hours of study and practice to master, more employers prefer to hire certified mechanics. Certification assures the employer that the employee is skilled in the latest repair procedures and is familiar with the most current diesel technology. Those with good communication and planning skills may advance to shop supervisor or service manager at larger repair shops or companies that keep large fleets. Others with good business skills go into business for themselves and open their own shops or work as freelance mechanics. Some master mechanics may teach at technical and vocational schools or at community colleges.

Earnings

Diesel mechanics' earnings vary depending upon their region, industry (trucking, construction, railroad), and other factors. Technicians in the West and Midwest tend to earn more than those in other regions, although these distinctions are gradually disappearing. Diesel mechanics who work at hourly rates can make significantly more money through overtime pay. Mechanics who work for companies that must operate around the clock, such as bus lines, may work at night, on weekends, or on holidays and receive extra pay for this work. Some industries are subject to seasonal variations in employment levels, such as construction. Beginning salaries start in the low $20s, but experienced diesel mechanics can earn $30,000 to $40,000 a year, according to NATEF.

Mechanics employed by firms that maintain their own fleets, such as trucking companies, can have earnings that average over $32,000 per year, at a 40-hour week. Those who put in longer hours or work during periods when they are eligible for extra pay may make substantially more. Among mechanics who service company vehicles, the best paid are usually those employed in the transportation industry. Diesel mechanics employed by companies in the manufacturing, wholesale, and retail trades and service industries have average hourly earnings that may be as much as 10 percent lower than transportation diesel mechanics. Mechanics working for construction companies during peak summer building seasons earn up to $1,000 a week.

Many diesel mechanics are members of labor unions, and their wage rates are established by contracts between the union and the employer. Benefits packages vary from business to business. Mechanics can expect health insurance and paid vacation from most employers. Other benefits may include dental and eye care, life and disability insurance, and a pension plan. Employers usually cover a mechanic's work clothes through a clothing allowance and may pay a percentage of hand tools purchases. An increasing number of employers pay all or most of an employee's certification training if he or she passes the test. A mechanic's salary can increase by yearly bonuses or profit sharing if the business does well.

Work Environment

Depending on the size of the shop and whether it's a trucking or construction company, government, or private business, diesel mechanics work with anywhere from two to 20 other mechanics. Most shops are well lighted and well ventilated. They can be frequently noisy due to running trucks and equipment. Hoses are attached to exhaust pipes and led outside to avoid carbon monoxide poisoning.

Minor hand and back injuries are the most common problem for diesel mechanics. When reaching in hard-to-get-at places or loosening tight bolts, mechanics often bruise, cut, or burn their hands. With caution and experience most mechanics learn to avoid hand injuries. Working for long periods of time in cramped or bent positions often results in a stiff back or neck. Diesel mechanics also lift many heavy objects that can cause injury if not handled cautiously; however, most shops have small cranes or hoists to lift the heaviest objects. Some may experience allergic reactions to the variety of solvents and oils frequently used in cleaning, maintenance, and repair. Shops must comply with strict safety procedures to help employees avoid accidents. Most mechanics work between 40- and 50-hour workweeks, but may be required to work longer hours when the shop is busy or during emergencies. Some mechanics make emergency repairs to stranded, roadside trucks or to construction equipment.

Outlook

With diesel technology getting better (smaller, smarter, and less noisy), more light trucks and other vehicles and equipment are switching to diesel engines. Diesel engines already are more fuel-efficient than gasoline engines. This increase in diesel-powered vehicles, together with a trend toward increased cargo transportation via trucks, will create jobs for highly skilled diesel mechanics. Less skilled workers will face tough competition. The industry predicts it will need to replace 20 percent of its workforce by the end of the 20th century due to those retiring and those who cannot keep up with the changing technology. Also, the increased reliance by businesses on quick deliveries has increased the demand on trucking companies. Many businesses maintain lower inventories of materials, instead preferring to have items shipped more frequently. The increased demand on trucking companies translates to an increased demand for people who can repair and maintain trucks. In 1990, there were 268,000 diesel mechanics in the United States, according to the Bureau of Labor Statistics. That number is expected to grow to 326,000 by 2006.

Diesel mechanics enjoy good job security. Fluctuations in the economy have little effect on employment in this field. When the economy is bad, people service and repair their trucks and equipment rather than replace them. Conversely, when the economy is good more people are apt to service their trucks and equipment regularly as well as buy new trucks and equipment.

The most jobs for diesel mechanics will open up at trucking companies that hire mechanics to maintain and repair their fleets. Construction companies are also expected to require an increase in diesel mechanics to maintain their heavy machinery, such as cranes, earthmovers, and other diesel powered equipment.

For More Information

Automotive Service Industry Association (ASIA)
25 Northwest Point Boulevard, #425
Elk Grove Village, IL 60007
Tel: 847-228-1310
Web: http://www.aftmkt.com/asia

For information on accreditation and testing, contact:

Inter-Industry Conference on Auto Collision Repair (I-CAR)
3701 Algonquin Road, Suite 400
Rolling Meadows, IL 60008
Tel: 800-ICAR USA
Web: http://www.i-car.com

For more information on the automotive parts industry contact:

National Automotive Technicians Education Foundation (NATEF)
13505 Dulles Technology Drive
Herndon, VA 20171-3421
Tel: 703-713-0100
Web: http://www.natef.org

National Institute for Automotive Service Excellence
13505 Dulles Technology Drive, Suite 2
Herndon, VA 20171-3421
Tel: 703-713-3800
Web: http://www.asecert.org

Pittsburgh Diesel Institute
111 Business Route 60
Moon Township, PA 15108
Tel: 800-875-5963
Web: http://www.nauticom.net/www/pdi/pdi.htm

Flight Attendants

School Subjects
Psychology
Speech

Personal Skills
Communication/ideas
Helping/teaching

Work Environment
Primarily indoors
Primarily multiple locations

Minimum Education Level
High school diploma

Salary Range
$12,000 to $19,000 to $40,000

Certification or Licensing
None available

Outlook
Faster than the average

Overview

Flight attendants are responsible for the safety and comfort of airline passengers from the initial boarding to disembarkment. They are trained to respond to emergencies and passenger illnesses. Flight attendants are required on almost all national and international commercial flights.

History

Although the first commercial passenger flights occurred as early as 1911, early airplane flights were not very comfortable. Airplanes were unstable, relatively small and could not achieve very high altitudes. It was also difficult to operate passenger service at a profit. In the United States, the commercial aviation industry did not take off until the Kelly Air Mail Act of 1925, which encouraged the growth of the first commercial airlines. For many years, commercial airlines prospered because of profits from their airmail business; the government, in an effort to encourage passenger travel, offered airlines subsidies to lower the price of passenger tickets.

Concerns about the safety of airplanes kept many people from flying. In 1926, however, the Air Commerce Act, which established regulations and requirements for pilots and airlines and also defined an airway system, improved consumer confidence in the airline industry. The famous flight of Charles Lindbergh the following year did much to promote public excitement about flying. Improvements such as stronger engines, better radio and navigational aids, and weather forecasting techniques were making flights safer. An important advancement in commercial air travel came with the development of the pressurized cabin. This meant that passengers could fly unaffected by the thin air of higher altitudes. As more people began to fly, the airlines sought ways to make flights even safer, more comfortable, and more enjoyable for the passenger. United Airlines was the first to offer special service to passengers in flight. In 1930, they hired graduate nurses to tend to their passengers' comfort and needs. They were called stewardesses, after the similar position on cruise ships. Soon after, other airlines added stewardesses to their flights as well. At first, stewardesses performed many functions for the airlines, often acting as mechanics, refueling airplanes, loading passenger luggage and equipment necessary for the flight, as well as cleaning the interior of the airplane. But as airplanes grew larger and the numbers of passengers increased, these positions were filled by specialized personnel, and the stewardesses' responsibilities were devoted to the passengers. Stewardesses also began preparing and serving meals and drinks during flights.

The increasing growth and regulation of the airline industry brought still more duties for the flight attendant. Flight attendants began to instruct passengers on proper safety procedures, and they were required to make certain that safety factors were met before takeoff.

In the early years, most flight attendants were women, and the airlines often required that they remain unmarried in order to retain their jobs. Airlines also instituted age, height, and weight restrictions. Flight attendants were expected to provide a glamorous and pleasant image for airlines. During this time, employee turnover was very high. However, as the role of the flight attendant became more important and as regulations required them to perform more safety-oriented tasks, the image of the flight attendant changed as well. Because training flight attendants was expensive, the airlines began to offer better benefits and other incentives and removed some of their employee restrictions. Experience was also rewarded with higher pay, better benefits, and seniority privileges given according to the number of years worked. More and more flight attendants were making a career with the airlines. The introduction of FAA regulations requiring at least one flight attendant for every 50 passengers gave even greater growth and job security to this career.

Today, flight attendants fill more positions than any other airline occupation. The more than 75,000 flight attendants play a vital role in maintaining the safety and comfort of the skies. Many airlines are easing still more of their restrictions, such as age and weight limitations, as the role of the flight attendant has changed to require special training and skills.

The Job

Flight attendants perform a variety of preflight and inflight duties. At least one hour before takeoff, they attend a briefing session with the rest of the flight crew; carefully check flight supplies, emergency life jackets, oxygen masks, and other passenger safety equipment; and see that the passenger cabins are neat, orderly, and furnished with pillows and blankets. They also check the plane galley to see that food and beverages to be served are on board and that the galley is secure for takeoff.

Attendants welcome the passengers on the flight and check their tickets as they board the plane. They show the passengers where to store briefcases and other small parcels, direct them to their cabin section for seating, and help them put their coats and carry-on luggage in overhead compartments. They often give special attention to elderly or disabled passengers and those traveling with small children.

Before takeoff, a flight attendant speaks to the passengers as a group, usually over a loudspeaker. He or she welcomes the passengers and gives the names of the crew and flight attendants, as well as weather, altitude, and safety information. As required by federal law, flight attendants demonstrate the use of lifesaving equipment and safety procedures and check to make sure all passenger seatbelts are fastened before takeoff.

Upon takeoff and landing and during any rough weather, flight attendants routinely check to make sure passengers are wearing their safety belts properly and have their seats in an upright position. They may distribute reading materials to passengers and answer any questions regarding flight schedules, weather, or the geographic terrain over which the plane is passing. Sometimes they call attention to points of interest that can be seen from the plane. They observe passengers during the flight to ensure their personal comfort and assist anyone who becomes airsick or nervous.

During some flights, attendants serve prepared breakfasts, lunches, dinners, or between-meal refreshments. They are responsible for certain clerical duties, such as filling out passenger reports and issuing reboarding passes. They keep the passenger cabins neat and comfortable during flights. Attendants serving on international flights may provide customs and airport information and sometimes translate flight information or passenger instructions into a foreign language. Most flight attendants work for commercial airlines. A small number, however, work on private airplanes owned and operated by corporations or private companies.

Requirements

High School

Flight attendants need to have at least a high school education. A broad education is important to allow flight attendants to cope with the variety of situations they will encounter on the job. Beginning foreign language studies in high school will open up the possibility of working on international flights later.

Postsecondary Training

Applicants with college-level education are often given preference in employment. Business training and experience working with the public are also assets. Attendants employed by international airlines are usually required to be able to converse in a foreign language.

Most large airline companies maintain their own training schools for flight attendants. Training programs may last from four to six weeks. Some smaller airlines send their applicants to the schools run by the bigger airlines. A few colleges and schools offer flight attendant training, but these graduates may still be required to complete an airline's training program.

Airline training programs usually include classes in company operations and schedules, flight regulations and duties, first aid, grooming, emergency operations and evacuation procedures, flight terminology, and other types of job-related instruction. Flight attendants also receive 12 to 14 hours of additional emergency and passenger procedures training each year. Trainees for international flights are given instruction on customs and visa regulations and are taught procedures for terrorist attacks. Near the end of the training period, trainees are taken on practice flights, in which they perform their duties under supervision.

An on-the-job probationary period, usually six months, follows training school. During this time, experienced attendants pay close attention to the performance, aptitudes, and attitudes of the new attendants. After this period, new attendants serve as reserve personnel and fill in for attendants who are ill or on vacation. While on call, these reserve attendants must be available to work on short notice.

Other Requirements

Airlines in the United States require flight attendants to be U.S. citizens, have permanent resident status, or have valid work visas. In general, applicants must be at least 19 to 20 years old, although some airlines have higher minimum age requirements. They should be at least five feet, two inches tall in order to reach overhead compartments, and their weight should be in proportion to their height.

Airlines are particularly interested in employing people who are intelligent, poised, resourceful, and able to work in a congenial and tactful manner with the public. Flight attendants must have excellent health, good vision, and the ability to speak clearly. Young people who are interested in this occupation need to have a congenial temperament, a pleasant personality, and the desire to serve the public. They must be able to think clearly and logically, especially in emergency situations, and they must be able to follow instructions working as team members of flight crews.

Exploring

Opportunities for experience in this occupation are almost nonexistent until an individual has completed flight attendant training school. Interested persons may explore this occupation by talking with flight attendants or people in airline personnel offices. Airline companies and private training schools publish many brochures describing the work of flight attendants and send them out upon request.

Employers

The vast majority of flight attendants are employed by commercial airlines. A very small number of flight attendants work on company-owned or private planes.

Starting Out

Individuals who are interested in becoming flight attendants should apply directly to the personnel divisions of airline companies. The names and locations of these companies may be obtained by writing to the Air Transport Association of America. Addresses of airline personnel division offices can also be obtained from almost any airline office or ticket agency. Some major airlines have personnel recruiting teams that travel throughout the United States interviewing prospective flight attendants. Airline company offices can provide interested people with information regarding these recruitment visits, which are sometimes announced in newspaper advertisements in advance.

Advancement

A number of advancement opportunities are open to flight attendants. They may advance to positions as first flight attendant (sometimes known as the flight purser), supervising flight attendant, instructor, or airline recruitment representative. They may also have the opportunity to move up to chief attendant in a particular division or area. Although the rate of turnover in this field was once high, more people are making careers as flight attendants and competition for available supervisory jobs is very high.

Many flight attendants who no longer qualify for flight duty because of health or other factors move into other jobs with the airlines. These jobs may include reservation agent, ticket agent, or personnel recruiter. They may also work in the public relations, sales, air transportation, dispatch, or communications divisions. Trained flight attendants may also find similar employment in other transportation or hospitality industries such as luxury cruise ship lines.

Earnings

Beginning flight attendants earned an average of $12,800 per year in 1996. Those with six years of flying experience earned an average of about $19,000 while some senior flight attendants earned up to $40,000 a year. Wage and work schedule requirements are established by union contract. Most flight attendants are members of the Transport Workers Union of America or the Association of Flight Attendants.

Flight attendants are limited to a specific number of flying hours. In general, they work approximately 80 hours of scheduled flying time and an additional 35 hours of ground duties each month. They receive extra compensation for overtime and night flights. Flight attendants on international flights customarily earn higher salaries than those on domestic flights. Most airlines give periodic salary increases until a maximum pay ceiling is reached. Flight assignments are often based on seniority, with the most senior flight attendants having their choice of flight times and destinations.

Airlines usually pay flight attendants in training either living expenses or a training salary. Companies usually pay flight attendants' expenses such as food, ground transportation, and overnight accommodations while they are on duty or away from home base. Some airlines may require first-year flight attendants to furnish their own uniforms, but most companies supply them.

Fringe benefits include paid sick leave and vacation time, free or reduced air travel rates for attendants and their families, and, in some cases, group hospitalization and life insurance plans and retirement benefits.

Work Environment

Flight attendants are usually assigned to a home base in a major city or large metropolitan area. These locations include New York, Chicago, Boston, Miami, Los Angeles, San Francisco, and St. Louis. Some airlines assign attendants on a rotation system to home bases, or they may give preference to the requests of those with rank and seniority on bids for certain home bases. Those with the longest records of service may be given the most desirable flights and schedules.

Flight attendants need to be flexible in their work schedules, mainly because commercial airlines maintain operations 24 hours a day throughout the entire year. They may be scheduled to work nights, weekends, and on holidays, and they may find that some of their allotted time off occurs away from home between flights. They are often away from home for several days at a time. They work long days, but over a year's time, a flight attendant averages about 156 days off, compared with 96 days off for the average office worker.

The work performed by flight attendants may be physically demanding in some respects. For most of the flight, they are usually on their feet servicing passengers' needs, checking safety precautions, and, in many cases, serving meals and beverages. Working with the public all day can be draining.

Flight attendants are the most visible employees of the airline, and they must be courteous to everyone, even passengers who are annoying or demanding. The occupation is not considered a hazardous one; however, there is a certain degree of risk involved in any type of flight work. Flight attendants may suffer minor injuries as they perform their duties in a moving aircraft.

The combination of free time and the opportunity to travel are benefits that many flight attendants enjoy. For those who enjoy helping and working with people, being a flight attendant may be a rewarding career.

Outlook

Nearly 132,000 professionally trained flight attendants are employed in the United States. Commercial airlines employ the vast majority of all flight attendants, most of whom are stationed in the major cities that serve as their airlines' home base.

Employment opportunities for flight attendants are predicted to grow faster than average through the year 2006. Population growth and higher income are likely to increase the numbers of airline passengers. To meet the needs of the traveling public, airline companies are using larger planes and adding more flights. Because federal regulations require at least one attendant on duty for every 50 passengers aboard a plane, this means there will be many more openings for flight attendants.

Finding employment as a flight attendant is highly competitive, and since job restrictions at airlines have been abolished, the once high rate of turnover for flight attendants has declined. Even though the number of job openings is expected to grow, airlines receive thousands of applications each year. Students interested in this career will have a competitive advantage if they have at least two years of college and prior work experience in customer relations or public contact. Courses in business, psychology, sociology, geography, speech, communications, first aid and emergency medical techniques such as CPR, and knowledge of foreign languages and cultures will make the prospective flight attendant more attractive to the airlines.

For More Information

For information on educational and career opportunities, please contact:

Air Transport Association of America
1301 Pennsylvania Avenue, NW
Washington, DC 20004
Web: http://www.air-transport.org/

Federal Aviation Administration
U.S. Department of Transportation
800 Independence Avenue, SW
Washington, DC 20591
Web: http://www.faa.gov/

For career books and information about high school student membership, national forums, and job fairs, contact:

Aviation Information Resources, Inc.
1001 Riverdale Court
Atlanta, GA 30337
Tel: 800-AIR-APPS
Web: http://www.airapps.com

Flight Attendant Corporation of America
Web: http://www.flightattendantcorp.com/

Helicopter Pilots

School Subjects

Mathematics
Physics

Personal Skills

Leadership/management
Technical/scientific

Work Environment

Primarily indoors
Primarily multiple locations

Minimum Education Level

High school diploma

Salary Range

$33,700 to $47,000 to $72,500

Certification or Licensing

Required for commercial pilots

Outlook

About as fast as the average

Overview

Helicopter pilots serve in a wide range of fields, from medicine to communications, and are employed by both the government and private industry. They are vital in emergency situations, in gathering information, and in transporting people and cargo short distances. Helicopter pilots are employed across the United States and in other countries, and even in remote places throughout the world. (Also See *Pilots*.)

The Job

Helicopter pilots perform duties in medical evacuation, police and fire fighting work, forestry, construction, communications, agriculture, and offshore oil exploration. They may serve as air taxis, carry workers and supplies to oil rigs, rescue stranded flood victims, lift heavy materials to work sites, fly patients from one hospital to another, or give news and traffic updates for the media. Many, but not all, helicopter pilots who do police work are also law enforcement officers. Their work includes traffic regulation and survey, vehicle pursuits, surveillance, patrol, and search.

In addition to flying, helicopter pilots keep records of their aircraft's engine performance and file flight plans. Before and after flying they check the aircraft for problems and may even do repairs and general upkeep on the craft if they are licensed to do so.

While flying, helicopter pilots must monitor several dials and gauges to make sure the aircraft is functioning properly. They monitor changes in pressure, fuel, and temperature. Helicopter pilots also navigate using landmarks, compasses, maps, and radio equipment.

Requirements

Although helicopter pilots are not required to have a college degree, college credentials can lead to promotions and better jobs. Helicopter pilots may receive training in flying schools (which can be expensive) where they study the theory of flying, weather, radio, navigation, and Federal Aviation Administration (FAA) Regulations. They also receive flight training.

Most of these pilots learn to fly as officers in the army. (For officers, a college degree is required.) To become licensed as a commercial helicopter pilot, a military pilot must pass the FAA military competency exam.

Good judgment, emotional balance, and the ability to think and act under pressure are ideal personal characteristics for working as a helicopter pilot. To qualify, pilots must be at least 21 years of age and meet the physical requirements of employers.

Advancement

Seniority, hours of flight time, and type of aircraft are the key factors in getting promotions in the helicopter industry. When starting out, most helicopter pilots fly the smaller single-engine aircraft. As they gain experience and hours of flying time, they may fly larger helicopters and obtain higher paying jobs. Pilots employed by large companies may be promoted to chief pilot or aviation department manager.

Earnings

In 1996, commercial helicopter pilots made an average of $33,700 to $59,900 a year. Corporate helicopter pilots earned an average of $47,000 to $72,500. The rate of pay for helicopter pilots is based on their level of experience, the size and type of craft they fly, their responsibilities, region, and employer.

Most employers of helicopter pilots provide medical, dental, and life insurance as well as paid vacations of about three weeks. For performing special services, such as flying to remote areas, they receive bonuses.

Work Environment

Some helicopter pilots work overtime, extra hours, and both daytime and night shifts. The number of hours helicopter pilots work depends on the type of employment. Air taxi pilots and police helicopter pilots may work 40 hours a week. Those who do police work may work more than 40 hours a week. Agricultural, forestry, and fire pilots may also work long hours.

Inside helicopters, pilots must remain seated in the cramped space for hours at a time. There is often mental stress involved in the constant alertness and concentration necessary for monitoring the craft's gauges and reading instruments. Fire fighting and law enforcement pilots are exposed to potential bodily harm while agricultural and construction pilots may be exposed to harsh chemicals.

Outlook

The future of the helicopter industry is fair to good, growing by about 5 percent a year. Because many helicopter pilots who were trained during the Vietnam War will soon be retiring, jobs will be available. Helicopters are also being used increasingly in other fields and industries, which is creating additional job opportunities for pilots.

For More Information

Helicopter Association International
1619 Duke Street
Alexandria, VA 22314
Tel: 703-683-4646

Locomotive Engineers

School Subjects
Computer science
Technical/Shop

Personal Skills
Mechanical/manipulative
Technical/scientific

Work Environment
Primarily indoors
Primarily multiple locations

Minimum Education Level
Apprenticeship

Salary Range
$25,000 to $52,903 to $65,374

Certification or Licensing
Required by all states

Outlook
Little change or more slowly than the average

Overview

Locomotive engineers operate the diesel locomotive engines that pull all types of trains, including cross-country freight trains and passenger trains. They also work in switchyards, where freight cars are joined together or broken apart. A locomotive engineer is generally the highest union position to which a railroad worker can advance.

History

The first railroads were so rudimentary that they didn't really require engineers to run them; they consisted simply of cars full of coal that moved through mines on wooden rails. In 1803, Richard Trevithick, a British mining engineer, built a steam locomotive that was able to pull a short train of cars uphill at a coal mine railway in Wales. Steam locomotives were first tested in the United States beginning in 1825. Three years later, construction was started on the first common carrier railroad in the states—the Baltimore and Ohio. In December of 1830, an American-built locomotive hauled a train of cars on the tracks of the South Carolina Railroad. The railroad had truly come to America, and the job of the locomotive engineer was established.

The importance of railroads to the growth and rapid expansion of America is impossible to measure, and the romance of railroading is firmly entrenched in American history. Folk songs such as "Casey Jones" have immortalized the locomotive engineer. The real work of the engineer, however, is not as romantic as it may appear. Today's locomotive engineer is often part of a two- or three-person crew; the longtime tradition of five-person crews is dying as instruments become computerized and automated. Where assistant engineers helped to monitor instruments and signals, the engineer and conductor now share these responsibilities.

The Job

Road engineers run locomotives that transport passengers or freight. Before a run, they first look at their trip orders. They may discuss with the conductor instructions, timetables, and precautions for moving dangerous cargo. They check the locomotive, ensuring adequate amounts of fuel, sand, and water.

Engineers sit in the cab of a locomotive. During a run, they operate the throttle to start and accelerate the train, and the airbrakes to slow and stop it. They monitor gauges, dials, and meters that measure speed, fuel, temperature, battery charge, and air pressure in the brake line. They also watch for and obey signals, both along the track and those received by train radio, which indicate obstructions on the track, other train movements, and speed limits.

Locomotive engineers must be familiar with their routes, knowing where curves and bridges are and what the safest speeds are for traveling over them. They must be able to adjust speed gradually, without disturbing passengers or damaging cargo. They must also be aware of the content and nature of their train, because the number and kind of cars and whether they are empty or full affects the way the train reacts to speeding up, slowing down, and going on hills and curves.

Yard engineers work in the switchyards and run locomotives or switch engines that are used to move freight or passenger cars when trains are being broken up or put together for a run. Some engineers spend several years on yard work, and later take up freight or passenger service work. Most, however, spend their careers in one type of work or the other.

Requirements

High School

A high school diploma is usually necessary to be hired. High school students should concentrate on any shop classes they can take, including courses in mechanics, electronics, and computer science.

Postsecondary Training

Vacancies for positions as locomotive engineers are usually filled from within by workers who have experience in other aspects of railroad operation, such as brake operators or conductors. Most railroads require that their engineers be at least 21 years old. Beginning engineers undergo a six-month training program, which includes classroom, on-the-job, and simulator work. Major railroads generally have their own training schools and smaller railroads usually send their engineers to these schools as well. After completing the training, prospective engineers must pass a qualifying exam on airbrake systems, fuel economy, train handling techniques, and operating rules.

Other Requirements

Mechanical aptitude, good hand-eye coordination, manual dexterity, and accurate judgment of the speed and distance of moving objects are important. Finally, good hearing, eyesight, and color vision are necessary. Most employees require that engineers pass a physical examination and drug screening tests before being hired. Also, if at any time they fail to meet the necessary health requirements, they may be restricted to working in only certain types of service.

Exploring

Finding general information about trains and railroads is usually easy, as there is an abundance of information in local libraries and on the Internet. Hobbyists often become experts on a particular aspect of the railroads, such as types of cars used and locomotive engine history. Many hobbyists post Web pages on the Internet with interesting information. Also, hobby shows are still held in many places throughout the country and most hobbyists can tell anyone who asks a lot about railroads and their history. Students may also learn more about the job by arranging an interview with an engineer or by visiting a work site. Railroads crisscross the country, so there should at least be a track near you. Visiting a work site may be possible only for those who live near a headquarters or one of the many regional offices all over the country. Look in the yellow pages to see if any railroads are listed in your area. Or ask your local chamber of commerce which railroads serve your area and how to contact them.

Employers

Locomotive engineers may be employed by passenger lines or freight lines. They may work for one of the major railroads, such as Burlington Northern Santa Fe, Norfolk Southern, CSX, or Atchison-Topeka-Santa Fe, or they may work for one of the 500 smaller short line railroads across the country. Many of the passenger lines today are commuter lines located near large metropolitan areas. Locomotive engineers who work for freight lines may work in a rural or an urban area and travel more extensively than the shorter, daily commuter routes that passenger locomotive engineers travel. There were 83,000 rail transportation workers in 1996, according to the Bureau of Labor Statistics, 21,000 of which were locomotive engineers.

Starting Out

The only way to become a locomotive engineer is to start at a lower level and work up to the position. For many railroads, union/railroad agreements dictate the specific steps required to become a locomotive engineer; many locomotive engineers started out as conductors. To find an entry-level job with a railroad, aspiring engineers should apply directly to railroad employment offices, as well as to state employment offices.

Advancement

When engineers first begin their careers, they are placed on the "extra board." Extra board engineers work only when the railroad needs substitutes for regular workers. They often have to work many years in this capacity before they accumulate enough seniority to get a regular assignment. Seniority rules may also allow workers with more years spent on the job to select the type of assignment they desire. It is possible for an experienced engineer to advance into a supervisory position, such as supervisor of engines for the road, but the number of such positions is small.

Earnings

Earnings for locomotive engineers are negotiated in union contracts. The earnings depend on the class of locomotive operated, the kind of service in which the engineer is employed, and the amount of seniority he or she has. According to 1997 figures from the National Railroad Labor Conference, annual earnings for engineers ranged from an average of $52,903 for yard freight engineers to $65,374 for passenger engineers.

The beginning engineer's salary may be quite varied, because he or she must serve time on the extra board, rather than have a regular, steady assignment. Typically, full-time employees have higher earnings than those on the extra board.

On many routes, the amount an engineer may earn in a single month is governed by mileage limitations agreed upon by the unions and the railroad companies. Whenever an engineer on one of these routes reaches the top number of miles permitted during a month, another engineer, usually an extra board worker, is assigned to take over for the rest of the month.

Engineers receive paid vacations, sick leave, life and health insurance, railroad retirement pensions, and other benefits.

Work Environment

The conditions of work for engineers are governed by the type of job. The yard engineer generally works a standard 40-hour week, in one location. The road engineer, while on the extra board, may work irregular hours and be on call for 24 hours, seven days a week. Even those with regular assignments rarely have what would be considered regular workweeks, since trains run at all hours of the day and night. All road engineers are away from home—at their own expense—a certain amount of the time. Both road and yard engineers may work Sundays, nights, and holidays.

There is a certain amount of danger in the job from accidents, although modern communications such as train telephones and better equipment such as continuously welded rails have reduced the number of casualties.

The work is confining, and movement is limited in the cab of the engine. An engineer may have to sit at a throttle for many miles controlling a locomotive's speed and efficiency. However, he or she must stay alert and attentive and may be required to act instantly if an obstruction appears on the track. The position carries with it a high degree of responsibility, particularly in passenger service. Many engineers enjoy the travel that goes along with the job. They get the opportunity to see the American cities and countryside in a more extensive manner than most people.

Outlook

There are very few locomotive engineers—fewer than 22,000 in the entire United States—and it is expected that the number of job openings in this field will be extremely limited in the near future. However, while the Bureau of Labor Statistics predicts a decline for all other railroad transportation workers, it does expect some limited growth in the number of locomotive engineer positions. Locomotive engineers are essential to a train's operation and the position has not suffered the cuts that assistant engineers and brake operators have, for example. Also, demand for railroad freight service is expected to increase as the economy expands. Still, most openings will arise from the need to replace workers who leave the occupation.

For More Information

For information about the railroad industry and on the career of locomotive engineers, contact:

Association of American Railroads
50 F Street, NW
Washington, DC 20001
Tel: 202-639-2100

Brotherhood of Locomotive Engineers
Standards Building, Mezzanine Floor
1370 Ontario Street
Cleveland, OH 44113
Tel: 216-241-2630

Merchant Mariners

School Subjects

Computer science
Technical/Shop

Personal Skills

Following instructions
Mechanical/manipulative

Work Environment

Indoors and outdoors
Primarily multiple locations

Minimum Education Level

Some postsecondary training

Salary Range

$9,100 to $31,200 to $78,000

Certification or Licensing

Recommended

Outlook

Little change or more slowly than the average

Overview

The merchant marine is that part of the maritime trade industry concerned with transporting cargo (and sometimes passengers) from place to place via water routes; it is also known as the commercial shipping industry. *Merchant mariners* operate ships and other water vessels on domestic and international waters. Workers on these ships are divided into three crews: the *deck crew,* which handles navigation and cargo operations; the *engine crew,* which oversees the generating system that propels the ship; and the *steward department,* which sees to meals and living quarters. Each crew is commanded by a designated officer.

History

Merchant shipping is an old industry, having developed out of the need and desire to trade and travel. In the early days of the American colonies, commercial shipping was very important. Deep-water rivers and channels provided perfect launching sites for water vessels built by craftspeople who emigrated from other countries.

Between 1800 and 1840, U.S. ships carried more than 80 percent of the country's commerce with other nations. The first steamship crossed the Atlantic Ocean in 1819, and large iron ships began to be built in the mid-1800s. With the mass production of these iron ships, trade increased and Great Britain dominated the industry through the end of the century. Most U.S. trade was carried by foreign ships.

The merchant marine has always been a private industry, but during times of war the industry has been relied upon by the government to help in a military capacity. The maritime industry benefits during wartime because the country's defense department contracts shipbuilders and merchant mariners to serve as auxiliaries to the military. In fact, the end of the world wars caused a depression in U.S. merchant shipping. During World War II the U.S. Merchant Marine Academy was established at Kings Point, New York, to offer training for merchant officers (it didn't admit women until 1974). There are now six maritime academies in the United States.

Since the 19th century the size, speed, and carrying capacities of nonmilitary transport ships have increased greatly. The various types of merchant marine vessels—including supertankers, freighters, barges, and container ships—now carry millions of tons of food, machinery, and petroleum across the waters each day under the flags of many countries.

Despite such advancement, however, much has changed in the business since colonial days. Today, U.S. merchant shipping continues to lag behind that in other nations because shipbuilding and operating costs are much higher here than elsewhere. And because passenger liner traffic has declined, the major type of merchant vessel today is the cargo ship.

The Job

Just as with land-based businesses, workers on merchant marine vessels can be categorized into various departments. In this industry we have the deck, engine, and steward departments, each overseen by officers. Whatever your ability and ambition, there could be a job in the merchant marine for you: captain, cook, mate, deckhand, electrician, or baker, for example.

The *captain,* or *master,* is in command of the vessel and is responsible for navigation, discipline, and the safety of the passengers, crew, and cargo. Captains set course and speed, maneuver the vessel to avoid hazards, and locate the vessel's position using navigation aids, celestial observations, and charts. The captain is also the sole representative of the vessel's owner and arranges organizational assignments of duties for the vessel's operation, navigation, and maintenance with the chief mate.

The deck department consists of the following personnel. The *chief mate,* also known as the *first mate* or *chief officer*, acts as the captain's first assistant. He or she is in charge of all cargo planning and deck work and assists with navigation, discipline, and maintaining order. The *second mate* is in charge of the maintenance of all navigating equipment and charts. *Third mates* are responsible for the maintenance of lifeboats and fire-fighting equipment; they are in charge of all signaling equipment and assist with cargo work. Mates usually stand watch at the navigating bridge for four hours at a time.

The *radio officer* performs all duties required for the operation, maintenance, and repair of radio and other electronic communications devices. Radio officers maintain depth-recording equipment and electronic navigational aids such as radar and loran (long-range navigation). They also receive and record time signals, weather reports, position reports, and other data.

The *boatswain,* or *bosun,* is in charge of the deck crew. He or she carries out orders for work details as issued by the chief officer, directs maintenance tasks such as chipping and painting, splices rope and wire for rigging, and handles lifeboats and canvas coverings.

Workers known as *able seamen* or *deckhands* perform general duties such as rigging cargo booms and readying gear for cargo loading or unloading. They stand watch and must be qualified as lifeboatmen, able to take charge of a lifeboat crew. Able seamen also steer the vessel by handling its wheel under the direction of the officer on watch (this duty is usually carried out by the quartermaster, or helmsman, on noncommercial ships). Ordinary seamen learn and assist in performing the duties of an able seaman by cleaning, chipping, painting, and washing down the vessel. They also coil and splice rope.

The engine department is made up of the following workers. The *chief engineer* is in charge of all propulsion machinery, auxiliaries, and power-generating equipment. He or she keeps logs on machinery performance and fuel consumption and is responsible for machinery repairs. The *first assistant engineer* is responsible for the maintenance of lubricating systems, electrical equipment, and engine-room auxiliaries. The *second assistant engineer* is responsible for fuel and water, supervises tank soundings, and keeps records of fuel and water consumption. He or she may be responsible for the operation of the vessel's boilers, boiler-room equipment, the feed water system, pumps, and condensers. The *third assistant engineer* supervises the operation and maintenance of engine-room auxiliaries and the vessel's pumps.

Electricians repair and maintain all electric motors and electrical circuits. *Wipers* keep the engine rooms clean by wiping down machinery, and oilers lubricate the moving parts of mechanical equipment throughout the vessel. *Firer-watertenders* take care of the boilers to keep the steam pressure constant.

They regulate the amount of water in boilers, check gauges, control the flow of fuel, and see to the operation of evaporators and condensers. On newer, automated vessels, the ratings of oilers and firer-watertenders have been combined, and these workers may be known as deck-engine mechanics.

The steward department maintains the crew's living quarters and prepares meals. The *chief steward* supervises food preparation and the operation and maintenance of living quarters and mess halls. Tasks include establishing and maintaining inventory records of foodstuffs, linens, bedding, and furniture and preparing requisitions for voyage requirements. The chief steward also oversees the staff who work in the steward department.

The *chief cook* prepares all meals and, in conjunction with the chief steward, plans menus. He or she butchers meat and issues items from the vessel's refrigerators and storerooms. The *second cook and baker* bakes all bread and pies and prepares desserts, salads, and night lunches. He or she is responsible for the upkeep and safety of the galley. The *mess attendants* set tables, serve meals, and wash dishes. They also maintain clean passages, stairways, and corridors; make berths in officers' and crew quarters; and keep the radio room and the vessel's offices clean.

Requirements

High School

Mathematics and physics courses are good training for a number of nautical activities. Computer science will prepare you for the increasing use of high technology at sea, and physical education will get you in shape for the sometimes strenuous work on a ship.

Postsecondary Training

A good way to fulfill many requirements and also learn about the various types of shipboard work is to attend a maritime school, such as Massachusetts Maritime Academy, U.S. Merchant Marine Academy, or Maine Maritime Academy. Most students at these schools are required to take courses in computer science, English, history, math, biological sciences, and social sciences. To be accepted to a maritime academy, a good scholastic achievement record and test scores are important. Also considered are extracurricular activities, character and personality, and leadership potential. To attend the U.S. Merchant Marine Academy, students must be nominated by a U.S. congressperson.

All officers and captains must be licensed by the U.S. Coast Guard. To obtain the rank of captain, chief mate, or second mate, an applicant must hold documentary evidence of being a U.S. citizen. All must pass certain U.S. Public Health Service physical exams and U.S. Coast Guard regulations regarding years of service and size of vessel on which the applicant served. Deck officers must have full knowledge of navigation, cargo handling, and all deck department operations. The captain must have good judgment and must know admiralty law, foreign pilots' rules, and trends in world trade.

Applicants for positions of chief engineer and first, second, and third assistant must show evidence of citizenship and pass health exams. To fulfill experience requirements, an applicant must have graduated from the U.S. Naval Academy, U.S. Merchant Marine Academy, or U.S. Coast Guard Academy or have combined education with experience in very specified areas. Engineers must have full knowledge of diesel engines and marine boilers. Chief engineers usually have college engineer training or the equivalent.

Unlicensed crew in the deck department must show proof of a job to obtain a merchant mariner's document from the U.S. Coast Guard. They may not sail without this document. After a required one-year minimum period of service, ordinary seamen may apply to the coast guard for a license as an able seaman. After three years they may secure unlimited endorsement as able seamen. An able seaman must hold an endorsed merchant mariner document, pass a physical exam, and pass either an oral or a written exam of knowledge of shipping and seamanship. Crew working in the steward's department must carry a certificate from a medical officer of the U.S. Public Health Service.

Certification or Licensing

To be eligible to serve as a deck, engine, or radio officer, a seaman must have a license issued by the U.S. Coast Guard. Radio operators must have a first- or second-class radiotelegraph operator's license issued by the Federal Communications Commission. Further, they must pass a written exam on such subjects as laws regulating communications at sea, radio and telegraph operating practices, message traffic routing, and radio navigational aids.

Other Requirements

Ultimately, merchant mariners must like to work on board water vessels. If you have ambitions of becoming a captain or an officer, you'll need a sense of leadership, good academic standing, and determination, as competition for jobs is heavy. Engineers must have a desire to work with the vessel's operating machinery. On the other hand, deckhands and steward crew should know that they want more general work. Naturally, the cooks and bakers should enjoy working in the kitchen. Newly hired deckhands usually learn their skills on the job.

Exploring

Assuming you are already accustomed to being on a boat, there are very few opportunities to explore this field before actually enrolling in a maritime program or applying at union halls or shipping companies. Beginners can hire on a vessel as ordinary seamen to see if they like working onboard. Individuals who already have some training or experience (for instance, as a cook, waiter, electrician, or engineer) might hire on for a voyage to try the experience. If near a port, an aspiring merchant mariner could visit a vessel in port by contacting a steamship company. Visiting coastal ports (e.g., in Maine or California) is a good idea.

If students decide to enroll at a maritime academy, further opportunities for exploration are offered there. For example, Massachusetts Maritime Academy offers a slow-speed diesel simulator, a modern training ship, and a cargo-handling simulator. Students go on a nine-week sea cruise each year, and they can expect to visit 12 to 15 foreign ports of call by graduation. California Maritime Academy has an 8,000-ton training ship and a diesel tanker; Maine Maritime Academy has 100 sailing crafts of various sizes. Also, there is a merchant marine museum at the U.S. Merchant Marine Academy.

Employers

The majority of merchant marine jobs are at private companies, although some are employed on government-owned ships. Others work on coastal freighters or on tugboats or barges on inland waterways. Naturally, jobs are concentrated in coastal areas.

Starting Out

An inexperienced person usually gets a first job at sea by applying at a union hiring hall in a major port. An applicant is given a shipping card on which is stamped the date of register. In the hiring hall, dispatchers announce job openings as ordered by shipping companies. The best-qualified worker who is longest out of work gets the job. New applicants may have to wait months to get jobs, and may have to keep in daily contact with the employment center. To become a higher-ranking merchant mariner, such as a captain or an officer, it is best to attend one of the state maritime academies.

Advancement

There are many advancement opportunities in the merchant marine, whether from ordinary seaman to able seaman or from third mate to chief mate. But in almost every rank, promotion depends on length of service, experience, and training, either formal or on the job. Seamen in the deck department advance along well-defined lines; thus, after applying for rating, they take the required examination.

In the engine department, a wiper may advance to any one of many jobs, provided legal qualifications are met. In the steward department, advancement is from messman, to utility man, to assistant cook, to chief cook, and finally to steward. The deck officer must start as third mate; after one year an individual is eligible to take second mate examinations. Second mates gradually work toward more responsible positions, with years of service and experience acquired.

Earnings

Wages vary according to the worker's rank and the size of the vessel. The Economic Research Institute cites $39,089 a year as the average salary in 1997 for a captain with one year of experience. The average salary increased with tenure ($55,843 for 12 years of experience and $68,123 for 24 years of experience). Ship mates with one year of experience averaged annual earnings of $16,260 a year, but that figure jumped to $20,071 with five years of experience and $23,079 a year with 10 years experience. Seamen with one year of experience averaged salaries of $15,319 a year; with five years of experience, they earned an average of $18,909 a year; and with 10 years of experience, their salaries averaged $21,746. In all of these occupations, salaries are increased dramatically by overtime and vacation pay.

Ship employees generally receive good benefits, which include free room and board while aboard ship. They receive bonuses when working in more dangerous situations (such as when there is dangerous cargo aboard), and they usually receive generous paid vacations, medical benefits, pensions, and disability pay.

Work Environment

Contrary to what many people think, working in the merchant marine doesn't mean that you sign up for duty in the navy or other military force. The merchant marine is a private industry, although vessels may be obligated to help the military in times of war.

Working on board a vessel is not as glamorous as it first may seem. Crews must be prepared to be away from home for extended periods and, although they travel throughout the world, the crew rarely has time to see much of the ports they visit. Merchant mariners on ocean vessels must be on their vessel during long periods and thus are away from home more often than other workers. However, they can earn long leaves between jobs. Unless they have been in the merchant marine for a number of years, many workers are hired for one journey at a time. Workers on rivers, canals, and the Great Lakes are more likely to find steadier work.

Merchant mariners usually share their living area with other crew members. While at sea, they are exposed to all kinds of weather, often cold and damp conditions. Most mid- and lower-ranking workers must stand watch for four hours at a time. Also, fire, collision, and sinking are all possible, so workers must be physically and psychologically prepared for such hazards.

Outlook

The employment outlook for merchant marine personnel is not very good, mainly because of foreign competition and changes in federal policy. Cargo rates and wages paid to U.S. merchant mariners are the highest in the world, but this keeps the industry small because shippers can send goods on cheaper foreign vessels. In addition, newer ships with more automated equipment can be operated with smaller crews.

The job market for merchant marine graduates has tightened since the Gulf War. There has been a slump in the industry, which is forcing shipping companies to downsize. Many graduates take work at onshore jobs related to the maritime industry, such as with shipping companies and vessel manufacturers. Others are taking nontraditional courses such as pollution control and riverboat management, to broaden their opportunities. All graduates, however, become members of the U.S. Naval Reserve, and many sign up for active duty in the navy.

It is anticipated that most job openings will occur as workers retire or leave the field for other reasons. Applicants can expect to face sharp competition for these jobs. Many experienced merchant mariners go long periods without work.

For More Information

U.S. Maritime Administration
U.S. Department of Transportation
400 7th Street, SW
Washington, DC 20590
Tel: 202-366-5812
Web: http://marad.dot.gov/

For information on academic requirements, contact schools that offer merchant marine training, including the following:

California Maritime Academy
PO Box 1392
Vallejo, CA 94590
Tel: 707-648-4222
Web: http://www.csum.edu/

U.S. Merchant Marine Academy
300 Steamboat Road
Kings Point, NY 11024
Tel: 516-773-5000
Web: http://www.usmma.edu/

Pilots

School Subjects

Mathematics
Physics

Personal Skills

Leadership/management
Technical/scientific

Work Environment

Primarily indoors
Primarily multiple locations

Minimum Education Level

High school diploma

Salary Range

$26,290 to $76,800 to $200,000

Certification or Licensing

Required by all states

Outlook

About as fast as the average

Overview

Pilots perform many different kinds of flying jobs. In general, pilots operate an aircraft for the transportation of passengers, freight, mail, or for other commercial purposes.

History

The age of modern aviation is generally considered to have begun with the famous flight of Orville and Wilbur Wright's heavier-than-air machine on December 17, 1903. On that day, the Wright brothers flew their machine four times and became the first airplane pilots. In the early days of aviation, the pilot's job was quite different from that of the pilot of today. As he flew the first plane, for instance, Orville Wright was lying on his stomach in the middle of the bottom wing of the plane. There was a strap across his hips, and to turn the plane, Wright had to tilt his hips from side to side.

Aviation developed rapidly as designers raced to improve upon the Wright brothers' design. During the early years of flight, many aviators earned a living as "barnstormers," entertaining people with stunts and by taking passengers on short flights around the countryside. Airplanes were quickly adapted to military use. Pilots soon became famous for their war exploits and for feats of daring and endurance as improvements in airplane designs allowed them to make transcontinental, transoceanic, or transpolar flights. As airplanes grew more complex and an entire industry developed, pilots were joined by copilots and flight engineers to assist in operating the plane.

The airline industry originated from the United States government-run air mail service. Pilots who flew for this service were praised in newspapers and their work in this new, advanced industry made their jobs seem glamorous. But during the Great Depression, pilots faced the threat of losing their high pay and status. The Air Line Pilots Association stepped in and won federal protection for the airline pilot's job. In 1978, when the airline industry was deregulated, many expected the pay and status of pilots to decrease. However, the steady growth of airlines built a demand for good pilots and their value remained high.

Today, pilots perform a variety of services. Many pilots fly for the military services. Pilots with commercial airlines fly millions of passenger and cargo flights each year. Other pilots use airplanes for crop-dusting, pipeline inspection, skydiving, and advertising. Many pilots provide instruction for flight schools. A great many pilots fly solely for pleasure, and many people own their own small planes.

The Job

The best known pilots are the commercial airline pilots who fly for the airlines. Responsible, skilled professionals, they are among the highest paid workers in the country. The typical pilot flight deck crew includes the *captain,* who is the pilot in command, and the *copilot,* or *first officer.* In larger aircraft, there may be a third member of the crew, called the *flight engineer,* or *second officer.* The captain of a flight is in complete command of the crew, the aircraft, and the passengers or cargo while they are in flight. In the air, the captain also has the force of law. The aircraft may hold 30 people or 300 or be completely loaded with freight, depending on the airline and type of operations. The plane may be fitted with either turbojet, turboprop (which have propellers driven by jet engines), or reciprocating propeller engines. An aircraft may operate near the speed of sound and at altitudes as high as 40,000 feet.

In addition to actually flying the aircraft, pilots must perform a variety of safety-related tasks. Before each flight, they must determine weather and flight conditions, ensure that sufficient fuel is on board to complete the flight safely, and verify the maintenance status of the aircraft. The captain briefs all crew members, including the flight attendants, about the flight. Pilots must also perform system operation checks to test the proper functioning of instrumentation, controls, and electronic and mechanical systems on the flight deck. Pilots coordinate their flight plan with airplane dispatchers and air traffic controllers. Flight plans include information about the airplane, the passenger or cargo load, and the air route the pilot is expected to take.

Once all preflight duties have been performed, the captain taxis the aircraft to the designated runway and prepares for takeoff. Takeoff speeds must be calculated based on the aircraft's weight. The aircraft systems, levers, and switches must be in proper position for takeoff. After takeoff, the pilots may engage an electrical device known as the autopilot. This device can be programmed to maintain the desired course and altitude. With or without the aid of the autopilot, pilots must constantly monitor the aircraft's systems.

Because pilots may encounter turbulence, emergencies, and other hazardous situations during a flight, good judgment and ability are extremely important. Pilots also receive periodic training and evaluation on their handling of in-flight abnormalities and emergencies and on their operation of the aircraft during challenging weather conditions. As a further safety measure, airline pilots are expected to adhere to checklist procedures in all areas of flight operations.

During a flight, pilots monitor aircraft systems, keep a watchful eye on local weather conditions, perform checklists, and maintain constant communication with the air traffic controllers along the flight route. The busiest times for pilots are during takeoff and landing. The weather conditions at the aircraft's destination must be obtained and analyzed. The aircraft must be maneuvered and properly configured to make a landing on the runway. When the cloud cover is low and visibility is poor, pilots rely solely on the instruments on the flight deck. These instruments include an altimeter and an artificial horizon. Pilots select the appropriate radio navigation frequencies and corresponding course for the ground-based radio and microwave signals that provide horizontal, and in some cases vertical, guidance to the landing runway.

After the pilots have safely landed the aircraft, the captain taxis it to the ramp or gate area where passengers and cargo are off-loaded. Pilots then follow "afterlanding and shutdown" checklist procedures, and inform maintenance crews of any discrepancies or other problems noted during the flight.

Pilots must also keep detailed logs of their flight hours, both for payroll purposes and to comply with Federal Aviation Administration (FAA) regulations. Pilots with major airlines generally have few nonflying duties. Pilots with smaller airlines, charter services, and other air service companies may be responsible for loading the aircraft, refueling, keeping records, performing minor repairs and maintenance, and arranging for more major repairs.

The chief pilot directs the operation of the airline's flight department. This individual is in charge of training new pilots, preparing schedules and assigning flight personnel, reviewing their performance, and improving their morale and efficiency. Chief pilots make sure that all legal and government regulations affecting flight operations are observed, advise the airline during contract negotiations with the pilots' union, and handle a multitude of administrative details.

In addition to airline pilots, there are various other types of pilots. *Business pilots,* or *executive pilots* fly for businesses that have their own planes. These pilots transport cargo, products, or executives and maintain the company's planes as well. *Test pilots,* though there are not many, are very important. Combining knowledge of flying with an engineering background, they test new models of planes and make sure they function properly. *Flight instructors* are pilots who teach others how to fly. They may teach in classrooms or provide inflight instruction, or both. Other pilots work as examiners, or check pilots. They may fly with experienced pilots as part of their periodic review; they may also give examinations to pilots applying for licenses.

Some pilots are employed in the following specialties: *photogrammetry pilots* fly planes or helicopters over designated areas and photograph the earth's surface for mapping and other purposes. *Facilities-flight-check pilots* fly specially equipped planes to test air navigational aids, air traffic controls, and communications equipment and to evaluate installation sites for such equipment. This testing is directed by a supervising pilot.

Requirements

High School

All prospective pilots must complete high school. A college-preparatory curriculum is recommended because of the need for pilots to have at least some college education. Science and mathematics are two important subjects to prospective pilots, who should also take advantage of any computer courses offered. As explained below, students can start pursuing their pilot's license while in high school.

Postsecondary Training

Most companies that employ pilots require at least two years of college training; many require applicants to be college graduates. Courses in engineering, meteorology, physics, and mathematics are helpful in preparing for a pilot's career. Flying can be learned in either military or civilian flying schools. There are approximately one thousand FAA-certified civilian flying schools, including some colleges and universities that offer degree credit for pilot training. Pilots leaving the military are in great demand.

Certification or Licensing

To become a pilot, certain rigid training requirements must be met. Although obtaining a private pilot's license is not difficult, it may be quite difficult to obtain a commercial license. Any student who is 16 or over and who can pass the rigid mandatory physical examination may apply for permission to take flying instruction. When the training is finished, a written examination must be taken. If prospective pilots pass the examination, they may apply for a private pilot's license. To qualify for it, a person must be at least 17 years of age, successfully fulfill a solo flying requirement of 20 hours or more, and check out in instrument flying and cross-country flying. Student pilots are restricted from carrying passengers; private pilots may carry passengers but may not receive any payment or other compensation for the piloting activities.

All pilots and copilots must be licensed by the FAA before they can do any type of commercial flying. An applicant who is 18 years old and has 250 hours of flying time can apply for a commercial airplane pilot's license. In applying for this license, a candidate must pass a rigid physical examination and a written test given by the FAA covering safe flight operations, federal aviation regulations, navigation principles, radio operation, and meteorology. The applicant also must submit proof that the minimum flight-time requirements have been completed and, in a practical test, demonstrate flying skill and technical competence to a check pilot. Before pilots or copilots receive an FAA license, they must also receive a rating for the kind of plane they can fly (single-engine, multi-engine, or seaplane) and for the specific type of plane, such as Boeing 707 or 747.

An instrument rating by the FAA and a restricted radio telephone operator's permit by the Federal Communications Commission (FCC) are required. All airline captains must have an air transport pilot license.

Applicants for this license must be at least 23 years old and have a minimum of 1,500 hours of flight time, including night flying and instrument time. All pilots are subject to two-year flight reviews, regular six-month FAA flight checks, simulator tests, and medical exams. The FAA also makes unannounced spot check inspections of all pilots.

Jet pilots, helicopter pilots, and agricultural pilots all have special training in their respective fields.

Other Requirements

Sound physical and emotional health are essential requirements for aspiring pilots. Emotional stability is necessary because the safety of other people depends upon a pilot remaining calm and level-headed, no matter how trying the situation. Physical health is equally important. Vision and hearing must be perfect; coordination must be excellent; heart rate and blood pressure must be normal.

Exploring

High school students who are interested in flying may join the Explorers (Boy Scouts of America) or a high school aviation club. At 16 years of age, they may start taking flying lessons. One of the most valuable experiences for high school students who want to be a pilot is to learn to be a ham radio operator. By so doing, they meet one of the qualifications for commercial flying.

Employers

The commercial airlines, including both passenger and cargo transport companies, are the primary employers of pilots. Pilots also work in general aviation, and many are trained and employed by the military.

Starting Out

A large percentage of commercial pilots have received their training in the armed forces. A military pilot who wants to apply for a commercial airplane pilot's license is required to pass only the Federal Aviation Regulations examination if application is made within a year after leaving the service.

Pilots possessing the necessary qualifications and license may apply directly to a commercial airline for a job. If accepted, they will go through a company orientation course, usually including both classroom instruction and practical training in company planes.

Those who are interested in becoming business pilots will do well to start their careers in mechanics. They may also have military flying experience, but the strongest recommendation for a business pilot's job is an airframe and powerplant (A and P) rating. They should also have at least 500 hours flying time and have both commercial and instrument ratings on their license. They apply directly to the firm for which they would like to work.

Advancement

Many beginning pilots start out as copilots. Seniority is the pilot's most important asset. If pilots leave one employer and go to another, they must start from the bottom again, no matter how much experience was gained with the first employer. The position of captain on a large airline is a high-seniority, high-prestige, and high-paying job. Pilots may also advance to the position of check pilot, testing other pilots for advanced ratings; chief pilot, supervising the work of other pilots; or to administrative or executive positions with a commercial airline (ground operations). They may also become self-employed, opening a flying business, such as a flight instruction, agricultural aviation, air-taxi, or charter service.

Earnings

Airline pilots are among the highest paid workers in the country. The 1996 average starting salary for airline pilots was about $15,000 at small turboprop airlines and $26,290 at larger, major airlines. Pilots with six years of experience made $28,000 a year at turboprop airlines and nearly $76,800 at the largest airlines. Senior captains on the largest aircraft earned as much as $200,000 a year. Salaries vary widely depending on a number of factors, including the specific airline, type of aircraft flown, number of years with a company, and level of experience. Airline pilots are also paid more for international and nighttime flights.

Pilots with the airlines receive life and health insurance and retirement benefits; if they fail their FAA physical exam during their career, they are eligible to receive disability benefits. Some airlines give pilots allowances for buying and cleaning their uniforms. Pilots and their families may usually fly free or at reduced fares on their own or other airlines.

Work Environment

Airline pilots work with the best possible equipment and under highly favorable circumstances. They command a great deal of respect. Although many pilots regularly fly the same routes, no two flights are ever the same. FAA regulations limit airline pilots to no more than 100 flying hours per month, and most work around 75 hours per month, with few nonflying duties. This is because the pilot's job may be extremely stressful. During flights, they must maintain constant concentration on a variety of factors. They must always be alert to changes in conditions and to any problems that may occur. They are often responsible for hundreds of lives besides their own, and they are always aware that flying contains an element of risk. During emergencies, they must react quickly, logically, and decisively. Pilots often work irregular hours, may be away from home a lot, and are subject to jet lag and other conditions associated with flying. Pilots employed with smaller airlines may also be required to perform other, nonflying duties, which increase the number of hours they work each month.

For other pilots who handle small planes, emergency equipment, and delivery or supply routes to remote and isolated areas, the hazards may be more evident. Dropping medical supplies in Somalia, flying relief supplies into war zones, or delivering mail to northern Alaska are more difficult tasks than most pilots face. Business pilot schedules may be highly irregular and they must be on call for a great portion of their off-duty time. Business pilots and most private and small plane pilots are also frequently called upon to perform maintenance and repairs.

Outlook

The employment prospects of airline pilots look very good into the next century. The airline industry expects passenger travel to grow by as much as 60 percent, and airlines will be adding more planes and more flights to accommodate passengers. The outlook is less favorable, however, for business pilots. The recession of the early 1990s caused a decrease in the numbers of business and executive flights as more companies chose to fly with smaller and regional airlines rather than buy and operate their own planes and helicopters. The position of flight engineer is slowly being phased out as more and more airlines install computerized flight engineering systems.

Competition is expected to diminish as the many pilots who were hired during the boom of the 1960s reach mandatory retirement age. In addition, because the military has increased its benefits and incentives, many pilots choose to remain in the service, further reducing the supply of pilots for civilian work. These factors are expected to create a shortage of qualified pilots.

The aviation industry remains extremely sensitive to changes in the economy. When an economic downswing causes a decline in air travel, airline pilots may be given furlough. Business flying, flight instruction, and testing of new aircraft are also adversely affected by recessions.

For More Information

Contact the following organizations for information on a career as a pilot:

Air Line Pilots Association, International
PO Box 1169
Herndon, VA 22070
Tel: 703-689-2270
Web: http://www.alpa.org/

Air Transport Association of America
1709 New York Avenue, NW
Washington, DC 20006
Tel: 202-626-4000

Federal Aviation Administration
Flight Standards Division
Fitzgerald Federal Building
John F. Kennedy International Airport
Jamaica, NY 11430

Future Aviation Professionals of America
4291 J Memorial Drive
Atlanta, GA 30032
Tel: 800-JET-JOBS

Public Transportation Operators

School Subjects

Mathematics
Speech

Personal Skills

Following instructions
Mechanical/manipulative

Work Environment

Primarily indoors
Multiple locations

Minimum Education Level

High school diploma

Salary Range

$24,044 to $32,094 to $44,595+

Certification or Licensing

Required by all states

Outlook

About as fast as the average

Overview

Public transportation operators include drivers of intercity buses, local commuter buses, and local transit railway systems, such as subways and streetcars. Drivers of local bus and railway systems run a predetermined route within a city or metropolitan area, transporting passengers from one designated place to another. Intercity bus drivers travel between cities and states, transporting passengers and luggage on more lengthy trips. Some public transportation operators are required to handle additional special duties, such as transporting disabled passengers. These drivers generally respond to individual requests.

History

In both the United States and Europe, public transportation systems were first developed in the 19th century. As early as 1819, there was a successful horse-drawn bus service in Paris. The idea was subsequently adopted by other major cities, such as New York and London.

The first subway system, initially four miles long, was opened in London in the 1860s. The railcars were powered by steam until 1890, when the system was converted to electricity. New York, Chicago, Paris, Budapest, and many other cities followed with their own subway systems. Streetcar, or trolley, lines and elevated tracks were also built around this time. The first electric-powered elevated train system opened in Chicago in 1895.

The 20th century began with a new vehicle for public transportation—the gasoline-powered bus. Various cities throughout the United States established bus services in the first decade of the century. Trucks fitted with seats and automobiles lengthened for increased seating capacity were among the first buses. As roads improved and better equipment became available, bus systems expanded.

Toward the middle of the 20th century, some transit systems came under the ownership of automotive- or oil-related businesses that had little interest in maintaining trolley lines. Around the same time, bus systems began to receive government assistance because of greater routing flexibility and other advantages. By the 1950s, buses had largely replaced the country's trolley lines. Subways and elevated tracks, however, stayed in service, as did a few of the trolley systems, notably in San Francisco. In the latter half of the 20th century, some American cities, such as Washington, DC, and San Francisco, built new subway systems, while others expanded their existing underground lines.

The Job

The work of an intercity bus driver commonly begins at the terminal, where he or she prepares a trip report form, and inspects the bus. Safety equipment, such as a fire extinguisher and a first-aid kit, as well as the vehicle's brakes, lights, steering, oil, gas, water, and tires are checked. The driver then supervises the loading of baggage, picks up the passengers, collects fares or tickets, and answers questions about schedules and routes.

At the final destination, the intercity driver oversees the unloading of passengers and baggage and then prepares a report on the trip's mileage, fares, and time, as required by the Interstate Commerce Commission (ICC). Another report must be completed if an accident or unusual delay occurs.

Intercity bus drivers may make only a single one-way trip to a distant city or a round trip each day, stopping at towns and cities along the route. Drivers who operate chartered buses typically pick up groups, drive them to their destination, and remain with them until it is time for the return trip.

Within a town, city, or extended urban area, local commuter bus drivers usually make scheduled stops every block or two. As passengers board the bus, the driver notes passes and discount cards; collects fares, transfers, tokens, or tickets; and issues transfers. Drivers in many cities check student or senior citizen identification cards to be certain that individuals qualify for discount fares. At the end of the day, drivers of local transit buses turn in trip sheets, which might include records of fares received, the trips made, and any delays or accidents during their shift.

In order to reduce the threat of armed robbery, local bus drivers in most major cities do not give change. Passengers instead deposit their exact fare or token in a tamper-resistant box, and the driver looks at the fare through a viewing window to make sure that the correct amount was paid. Some buses have electronic boxes that count the bills and coins and then display the total of the transaction.

Drivers of both intercity buses and local commuter buses must operate their vehicles carefully during trips. They are required to follow established schedules, but they must do so within the legal speed limits. Bus drivers are also responsible for regulating the interior lights and the heating and air-conditioning systems.

Drivers of subway, streetcar, and other local railway systems have many of the same duties as bus drivers. Subway/elevated train drivers control trains that transport passengers throughout cities and suburbs. They usually sit in special compartments at the front of the train from which they start, slow, and stop the train. Subway drivers obey the signals along their routes, which run underground, at surface levels, or elevated above ground.

Some operators announce stops over the loudspeaker, open and close doors, and make sure passengers do not get caught in the closing doors. Some drivers are assisted by other operators, who collect fares and transfers, open and close doors, and announce stops. In order to remain on schedule, drivers control train speed and the amount of time they spend at each train station. When train malfunctions or emergencies occur, drivers contact dispatchers and may have to evacuate passengers from the train cars.

In general, all public transportation operators must answer questions from passengers concerning schedules, routes, transfer points, and addresses. They are also required to enforce safety regulations, such as a ban on smoking, established by the transit company or the government.

Requirements

High School

While still in high school, prospective drivers should take English and speech classes to make them more effective communicators. Math classes might also be helpful in calculating fares and making change. Finally, a driver's education class would be a great start.

Postsecondary Training

Qualifications and standards for bus drivers are established by state and federal regulations. Federal regulations require drivers who operate vehicles designed to transport 16 or more passengers to obtain a commercial or chauffeur's license. In order to receive this license, applicants must pass a knowledge test and a driving test in the type of vehicle they will be operating.

Federal regulations state that intercity bus drivers must be at least 21 years old and in good general health. They must have good hearing and vision; be able to speak, read, and write English well enough to fill out reports, read signs, and talk to passengers; and pass both a written and driving test in the type of bus they wish to drive. A high school diploma is also required. Some companies require bus drivers to be 24 years of age and prefer previous truck or bus driving experience.

Most intercity bus companies and local transit systems give their driver trainees two to eight weeks of classroom and "behind-the-wheel" instruction. In the classroom, trainees learn U.S. Department of Transportation and company work rules, state and municipal driving regulations, and general safe driving practices. They also learn how to read schedules, determine fares, and keep records.

For subway operator jobs, local transit companies prefer that applicants be high school graduates and that they be at least 21 years old. Good vision and hearing and a clean driving record are necessary. For some subway systems, previous experience driving a bus is required. New operators are generally placed in training programs, including classroom and on-the-job training, that range from a few weeks to six months. At the end of the training program, operators must pass qualifying exams covering the operating system, troubleshooting, and emergency procedures.

Other Requirements

Good hand, foot, and eye coordination is important in this career. Because drivers are required to deal regularly with passengers, it is important that they be courteous. An even temperament and a cool head are also very important in driving in heavy or fast-moving traffic or bad weather conditions. Drivers should be able to stay alert and attentive to the task at hand. They must be dependable and responsible, since the lives of their passengers are literally in their hands.

Exploring

Any job that requires driving all day can provide important experience for the prospective public transportation operator. Possibilities include a part-time, summer, or full-time position as a truck or taxi driver. Some companies and stores hire pickup and delivery drivers.

It might also be possible to arrange to talk personally with a bus driver or subway operator. Persons already employed in this capacity can give a good, detailed description of the duties, pros, and cons of the position.

Employers

The majority of jobs for bus drivers exist in school systems; approximately three out of every four drivers are employed by a school system or a company that provides contract school bus service. The second largest group of drivers work for local transit systems, with the smallest portion working as intercity drivers. According to a 1996 Bureau of Labor Statistics report, there are about 12,000 subway and streetcar operators—located almost exclusively in major urban areas.

Starting Out

Those high school students interested in the field should directly contact public transportation companies as well as government and private employment agencies. Labor unions, such as the Amalgamated Transit Union, might know about available jobs. Positions for drivers are sometimes listed in the classified section of the newspaper.

After completing the training program, new drivers may be placed on probation for 30 to 90 days. During this time, they perform their jobs under careful supervision. Many new drivers are initially given only special or temporary assignments—for example, substituting for a sick employee or driving a charter bus to a sporting event. These new drivers may work for several years in these part-time, substitute positions.

Advancement

Advancement is usually measured by greater pay and better assignments or routes. For example, senior drivers may have routes with lighter traffic, weekends off, or higher pay rates. Although opportunities for promotion are limited, some drivers may be moved to supervisory or training positions. It is also possible to become a dispatcher—the person who assigns each driver a bus or train, determines whether the buses or trains are running on time, and sends out help when there is a breakdown or accident. A small number of managerial positions also exist. Experienced subway or streetcar operators, for example, may become station managers.

Earnings

Earnings for public local transportation operators vary by location and experience. According to the American Public Transit Association, in 1997 local transit bus drivers in cities with more than 2 million inhabitants were paid

$17 per hour on average by companies with over 1,000 employees. Companies with fewer than 1,000 employees paid on average $15 per hour. In smaller cities, bus drivers made an average of $14 per hour where populations ranged from 250,000 to 500,000. They made on average $12 per hour where populations were below 50,000. According to American Public Transit Association data, subway train drivers earned an average of $21 per hour.

Almost all public transportation operators belong to a union, such as the Amalgamated Transit Union or the Transport Workers Union. Wages and benefits packages are usually determined through bargaining agreements between these unions and the management of the transit system. Often, benefits include paid health and life insurance, sick leave, free transportation on their line or system, and as much as four weeks of vacation per year.

Work Environment

Most public transportation operators work about 35 to 40 hours per week. New drivers, however, often work part-time, though they may be guaranteed a minimum number of hours.

Driving schedules for intercity bus drivers may require working nights, weekends, and holidays. Drivers may also have to spend nights away from home, staying in hotels at company expense. Senior drivers who have regular routes typically have regular working hours and set schedules; however, others do not have regular schedules and must be prepared to work on short notice. The hours can range from six to ten hours a day and from three and a half to six days per week. The Department of Transportation restricts intercity bus drivers from working more than ten hours per day and more than 60 hours per week.

Local transit drivers and subway operators usually have a five-day workweek, with Saturdays and Sundays being considered regular workdays. Some of these employees work evenings and night shifts. Also, to accommodate commuters, some work "split shifts," such as four hours in the morning and four hours in the afternoon and evening, with time off in between.

The lack of direct supervision is one of the advantages of being a bus driver or subway operator. Intercity bus drivers may also find the travel to be a benefit. Disadvantages might include weekend, holiday, or night shifts, and, in some cases, being called to work on short notice. Drivers with little seniority may be laid off when business declines.

Although driving a bus is usually not physically exhausting, drivers are exposed to tension that comes from driving a large vehicle on heavily congested streets and from dealing with many types of passengers.

Outlook

The employment outlook for intercity bus and local transit operators is expected to grow as fast as the average for all occupations through the year 2006. As the population increases and local and intercity travel increases, ridership on local and intercity buses should likewise increase. Future government efforts to reduce traffic and pollution through greater funding of public transportation could also greatly improve job opportunities. In addition, thousands of job openings are expected to occur each year because of the need to replace workers who retire or leave the occupation. Because many of these positions offer relatively high wages and attractive benefits, however, job seekers may face heavy competition. Those who have good driving records and are willing to work in rapidly growing metropolitan areas will have the best opportunities.

The outlook for subway operators is expected to be very good. As more cities build new subway systems and add new lines onto existing systems, the need for subway operators will increase. Again, however, because of the attractive features of the job, competition may be intense.

For More Information

For salary information on public transit operators, contact:

American Public Transit Association
1201 New York Avenue, NW, Suite 400
Washington, DC 20005
Tel: 202-898-4000

For information on careers in public transportation, contact:

Transport Workers Union
80 West End Avenue
New York, NY 10023
Tel: 212-873-6000

Railroad Clerks

School Subjects

Business
Mathematics

Personal Skills

Communication/ideas
Following instructions

Work Environment

Primarily indoors
Primarily one location

Minimum Education Level

High school diploma

Salary Range

$19,000 to $28,500 to $44,000

Certification or Licensing

None available

Outlook

Decline

Overview

Railroad clerks perform the clerical duties involved in transacting business and keeping records for railroad companies. Their jobs may involve many different kinds of clerical work or only one or two specialized duties, depending on the size and type of their railroad company or location.

History

The modern era of railroading began in the early 1800s, when two Englishmen, Richard Trevithick and George Stephenson, perfected their versions of the steam locomotive. In the early days, railroads were largely short lines, and a few clerks could keep track of the trains' cargo and destinations. But as railroads expanded, both geographically and in the types of freight they could carry, clerks became essential to keep track of what was being hauled where, when it was needed, and who would pay for it. The railroad industry reached an historic climax on May 10, 1869, with the completion of the first transcontinental railway. The Union Pacific Railroad, building west from Nebraska, and the Central Pacific Railroad, building east from California, met at Promontory Point, Utah, where a golden spike was driven to set the merging rails.

Passenger and freight business on the nation's rail lines peaked in the 1920s and 1930s, then went into decline. Still, rail is an important method of transportation. For example, automobile manufacturers use the railroad more than any other means of transportation to ship completed automobiles. Other commodities, such as coal and farm products, still rely heavily on rail. The railroad system is now a complex, interconnecting network of some 200,000 miles of lines that serve all parts of the country. While computers have eliminated some clerical jobs, clerks are still needed to keep accurate records, compile statistics, and transact railroad business for the complex systems of freight, express, and passenger rail service.

The Job

Volumes of paperwork are necessary to keep accurate records and provide information on the business transactions of railroad companies. Railroad clerks are responsible for completing and maintaining this paperwork. They interact with customers of the railroad and railroad employees at all levels.

Traditionally, railroad clerks have been employed in railroad yards, terminals, freight houses, railroad stations, and company offices. However, as railroad companies have merged, and as computerization has increasingly been used, railroads have tended to consolidate much of their operation into a centralized location. As a result, most railroad clerks no longer work on-site in the terminals; instead, they work at the railroad's central office. The information they need from the various terminals, yards, and stations is transmitted to them via computer and TV camera.

Clerks may perform a variety of duties, depending upon the size of the company they work for and the level of seniority they have achieved. Railroad clerks employed on Class I "line-haul" railroads perform such clerical duties as selling tickets, bookkeeping, compiling statistics, collecting bills, investigating complaints and adjusting claims, and tracing lost or misdirected shipments. *Yard clerks* use information from records or other personnel to prepare orders for railroad yard switching crews. They also keep records of cars moving into or out of the yard.

Pullman car clerks assign and dispatch sleeping cars to railroad companies requesting them and assign Pullman conductors to trains. Dispatcher clerks schedule train crews for work, notify them of their assignments, and record the time and distance they work.

Train clerks record the exact time each train arrives at or leaves the station, compare those times with schedules, and inquire about reasons for delays. They also process other data about train movements. Railroad-maintenance clerks keep records about repairs being made to tracks or rights-of-way, including the location and type of repair and the materials and time involved.

A great deal of railroad business and income involves moving freight. *Documentation-billing clerks* prepare the billing documents that list a freight shipper's name, the type and weight of cargo, destination, charges, and so on. They total the charges, check for accuracy, and resolve discrepancies. *Demurrage clerks* compute charges for delays in loading or unloading freight, prepare bills for these charges, and send the bills to the shippers or receivers responsible for the delays. They also communicate with shippers and receivers about the time and place of shipment arrival and the time allowed for unloading freight before they levy any charges.

Revising clerks verify and revise freight and tariff charges on shipment bills. *Interline clerks* examine waybills and ticket sales records to compute the charges payable to the various carriers involved in interline business. *Accounts adjustable clerks* compute corrected freight charges from waybill data. *Voucher clerks* receive claims for lost or damaged goods and prorate the cost of the goods to the various carriers involved in an interline shipment. *Express clerks* receive packages from customers, compute charges, write bills, receive payments, issue receipts, and release packages to the proper recipients.

Secretaries, typists, stenographers, bookkeepers, and operators of business and computing machines constitute a second group of railroad clerical workers. All of these employees perform clerical duties that are similar to those performed in other types of business and industry.

Thousands of railroad clerks are employed in higher-level jobs that require technical skills and knowledge. Such workers might include collectors, who pursue uncollected bills; accountants, who are concerned with company financial transactions; and records and statistical clerks, responsible for statistical compilations on railroad traffic, employees, and other business details. In addition, these employees are also frequently responsible for compiling periodic reports for the federal government on railroad business, transactions, and operational traffic.

Requirements

High School

A high school education is the minimum educational requirement for most railroad clerk positions. Business, computer, and communications courses will be helpful to prospective railroad clerks. Typing class is a must.

Postsecondary Training

Students who have postsecondary training in accounting, office management, or computer applications may be in a better position to get hired as a railroad clerk than students with high school diplomas only. In many instances, companies also require that potential employees successfully pass clerical aptitude tests and be able to type 35 to 40 words per minute. Finally, because computers are now commonplace in the railroad industry, potential clerks will find that they need a certain degree of computer literacy.

Other Requirements

Patience and attention to detail are important for clerical workers, especially those whose work may be repetitious. For those clerks who must deal regularly with the public, a congenial disposition, a pleasant phone voice, and the ability to get along well with others are valued assets. For example, one major railroad, Norfolk Southern, outlines the following standards for successful candidates for clerk positions: "be responsible and reliable, able to make quick decisions and prioritize work; be energetic and able to handle inquiries with strong interpersonal skills and a customer focus."

Exploring

One way to observe the work performed by railroad clerks is to obtain a part-time or summer job with a railroad company as a messenger or office assistant. If a railroad job is not available, working in any sort of office setting might give the prospective clerk experience with clerical work such as typing, stenography, bookkeeping, and the operation of common office equipment.

Employers

Railroad clerks may be employed by passenger lines or freight lines. They may work for one of the major railroads, such as Burlington Northern Santa Fe, Norfolk Southern, CSX, or Atchison-Topeka-Santa Fe, or they may work for one of the 500 smaller short line railroads across the country. Clerks who work for a major railroad generally work in a large centralized office with many other workers. Railroad clerks may work in any part of the country, urban or rural. Clerks who are employed by commuter passenger lines work in large metropolitan areas.

Starting Out

Railroad companies frequently fill railroad clerical positions by promoting current office assistants, janitors, or messengers. Therefore, the job seeker is most likely to find entrance into the field via a lower-level job. Once accepted for employment with a railroad company, a person may be given a temporary appointment as an "extra" and listed for "extra board" work until such time as a regular job appointment becomes available.

Individuals interested in railroad clerical jobs may apply directly to the railroad companies or inquire about job application procedures through the union representing this group of employees. Newspaper advertisements may sometimes list openings for clerical employees.

Advancement

Seniority plays a key role in advancement within the railroad industry. Jobs with higher pay, better hours, and more responsibility almost always go to those workers who have put in many years with the company. Most clerks are designated trainees for a period of 14 to 90 days when they first begin working before they advance to full-fledged clerks.

Railroad clerks who have achieved a high level of seniority and who have proven their abilities are sometimes promoted to assistant chief clerks or to positions of higher administrative status. Clerks who continue their formal education and training in some field of specialization, such as accounting or statistics, may have opportunities for promotions into jobs as auditors or statisticians. Other advancement opportunities may include advancement to traffic agent, buyer, storekeeper, or ticket and station agent.

Earnings

Salaries for railroad clerks vary depending on union agreements, training, experience, job responsibilities, and the type of operation in which the employee works. In most cases, hourly wages are set by the agreement between the railroad and the union. In 1998, clerks represented by the Transportation Communications Union who worked for a major railroad started at around $28,500 a year. Those workers on the low end of the pay scale make between $19,500 and $20,800 annually, while those at the top end can make between $41,600 and $44,200.

Railroad employees are usually paid time and a half for any time worked over eight hours a day. Most railroad employees are given paid vacation, sick days, and holidays. Retired railroad workers receive pensions and retirement insurance from the federal Railroad Retirement Administration, which they pay into while they are working.

Work Environment

A 40-hour workweek is the typical schedule for railroad clerical employees in nonsupervisory positions. Individuals who have temporary appointments may have an irregular work schedule, depending on the type of railroad setting in which they are employed. Clerks are sometimes expected to be available to work in a three-shift operation. Many clerks work strictly during the day, though. The majority of these workers perform their duties in comfortable, well-lit offices or stations. Large company offices may be more elaborately furnished and equipped than those of smaller stations.

The work of railroad clerks is not considered hazardous or physically strenuous; much of it is done while sitting down. Some types of clerical work can be tedious and unexciting, however, and in some cases, can result in eyestrain. Some clerks have to interact with the public, either by phone or in person. These workers are exposed to various sorts of people, some of whom may be difficult to deal with.

Outlook

Railroad clerks have been hit hard by the overall decline in railroad business; in the last 15 years, the total number of clerks employed has decreased by 50 to 60 percent. The increasing use of electronic data processing and computers have also played a large part in the employment decline for these workers, as machines have come to do more and more of the freight bill processing and recording of information on freight movements and yard operations.

Although this decline in employment is expected to continue, some job opportunities are expected to become available each year for these workers. Job turnover in this occupational group is relatively high as a result of retirements and employees transferring to other fields.

For More Information

For general information on the railroad industry, contact:

Association of American Railroads
50 F Street, NW
Washington, DC 20001
Tel: 202-639-2555
Web: http://www.aar.org/

For information on the career of railroad clerk, contact:

Transportation Communications International Union
Three Research Place
Rockville, MD 20850
Tel: 301-948-4910

Railroad Conductors

School Subjects
Computer science
Technical/Shop

Personal Skills
Leadership/management
Mechanical/manipulative

Work Environment
Indoors and Outdoors
Multiple locations

Minimum Education Level
Apprenticeship

Salary Range
$16,000 to $28,496 to $62,169

Certification or Licensing
None available

Outlook
Decline

Overview

Railroad conductors supervise trains and train crews on passenger trains, on freight trains, or in the rail yards. They are responsible for keeping track of the train's operating instructions and of its makeup and cargo.

History

The word "conductor" is likely to conjure up an image of the man who calls "All aboard!" before a train leaves the station. In the early days of the railroad, this association was accurate. Today, however, railroad conductors are more than a passenger liaison. With today's smaller crews, conductors and engineers often make up the entire crew aboard a train.

On many early passenger trains, the railroad conductor's most important task was to see to the comfort and safety of the passengers. For the first conductors, this was no simple task. The earliest trains had seats bolted to platforms that looked much like today's flat cars. There were no roofs over those cars, and consequently passengers were exposed to the elements, such as rain and wind, and to flying sparks from the tender boxes of locomotives. More often than not, the conductor had to extinguish fires started by flying sparks on the train and in passengers' clothing.

By the late 1830s, as trains crossed the unsettled western areas of the United States, the conductor's job became even more difficult and dangerous. Outlaws frequently attacked trains or tore up tracks and damaged bridges. Once rail came to be a popular method of both passenger and freight transportation in the latter half of the 1800s and early 1900s, railroad companies had the means to improve the quality of their locomotives and trains.

As locomotives and trains became more complex machines, conductors became well-versed in all areas of train operation. They were required to know a lot about all aspects of a train, from the engines, cars, and cargo to the track and signal systems. Today's conductors are responsible for the proper functioning of the entire train.

The Job

Railroad conductors fall into two categories: *road conductors* and *yard conductors*. Within the category of road conductors are included conductors of both freight and passenger trains, although their duties vary somewhat. The conductor is in charge of the train in its entirety, including all equipment and the crew.

Before a freight or passenger train departs from the terminal, the road conductor receives orders from the dispatcher regarding the train's route, timetable, and cargo. He or she then confers with the engineer and other members of the train crew, if necessary. During the run, conductors may receive additional communication by radio, such as information on track conditions or the instruction to pull off at the next available stop. They then relay this information to the engineer via a two-way radio. Conductors also receive information about any operating problems while underway and may make arrangements for repairs or removal of defective cars. They use a radio or wayside phone to keep dispatchers informed about the status of the trip.

Conductors on freight trains are responsible for getting bills of lading, lists of cars in their train, and written orders from the station agent and dispatcher. They keep records of each car's content and eventual destination, and see to it that cars are dropped off and picked up along the route as specified. Both before and during the run, they inspect the cars to make sure everything is as it should be.

On passenger trains, conductors see to it that passenger cars are clean and that passengers are seated and comfortable. They collect tickets and cash and attend to the passengers' needs. At stops, they supervise the disembarking of the passengers and tell the engineer when it is safe to pull out of the station. If an accident occurs, conductors take charge and direct passengers and other crew members.

Yard conductors are usually stationed at a switching point or terminal where they signal the engineer and direct the work of switching crews who assemble and disassemble the trains. Based on a knowledge of train schedules, the yard conductor or yard foreman is responsible for seeing that cars destined to arrive at various points along one of many routes are put together and ready to leave on time. He or she sends cars to special tracks for unloading and sends other cars to tracks to await being made into trains. Conductors tell switching crews which cars to couple and uncouple and which switches to throw to divert the locomotive or cars to the proper tracks. Today, many yards are mechanized. In this case, yard conductors supervise the movement of cars through electronic devices.

All conductors perform strenuous, outside work in all weather conditions and travel extensively. Usually, conductors are required to work on-call, on an as-needed basis. Railroads expect conductors, as well as most of their other employees, to be available to work 24 hours a day, seven days a week in all weather conditions. A certain time period is allotted, usually 12 hours, from the time of call to report to work.

Requirements

High School

The high school student interested in becoming a conductor will benefit from taking as many shop classes as possible. Any course that teaches electrical principles is particularly helpful. Because on-board computers are increasingly used in this profession, computer training would be a plus. Finally, academic subjects such as English and speech are also important because conductors are required to write some reports and speak to fellow workers and passengers.

Postsecondary Training

Many conductors acquire the knowledge to assume their positions through years of practical experience in other positions on the railroad. Railroads prefer that applicants for these jobs have high school diplomas, but further education, outside of the railroad's training school, is not typically required. To be eligible for a conductor's position, applicants must have passed examinations testing their knowledge of signals, timetables, air brakes, operating rules, and related subjects.

Other Requirements

Conductors must pass an entrance-to-service medical examination and must pass further physicals at regular intervals. They are also required to take tests that screen for drug use. Conductors must be able to lift 80 pounds, as required when replacing knuckles that connect rail cars. Because conductors are responsible for overseeing the activities of the other crew members and for dealing with the public, they must be capable of assuming responsibility, directing the work activities of others, and acting as the railroad's representatives to passengers. A conductor must have a good working knowledge of the operation of the train and of its mechanical details. In addition, he or she must be self-sufficient and capable of occupying free hours because much of the time is spent away from home. Finally, it is important that conductors have good judgment skills, be dependable, and be able to make quick, responsible decisions.

Exploring

A visit to a rail yard might give the interested person some insight into the work of a yard conductor and into the operations of railroads in general. It might be possible to arrange to talk with a conductor who works on a freight train or a passenger train for further insight. It might even be possible to obtain summer or part-time work for a railroad company.

Many conductors have an engineering or mechanical background, so students may find it helpful to explore such areas in high school through vocational clubs or classes. The Junior Engineering Technical Society is a nationwide organization that provides training and competition for students in engineering and technical subject areas. Visit the JETS Web site at http://www.asee.org/jets for more information or talk to a guidance counselor to see if your school or a school in your area has a chapter that you can participate in.

Employers

Railroad conductors may be employed by passenger lines or freight lines. They may work for one of the major railroads, such as Burlington Northern Santa Fe, Norfolk Southern, CSX, or Atchison-Topeka-Santa Fe, or they may work for one of the 500 smaller short line railroads across the country. Many of the passenger lines today are commuter lines located near large metropolitan areas. Railroad conductors who work for freight lines may work in a rural or an urban area and will travel more extensively than the shorter, daily commuter routes passenger railroad conductors make. There were 83,000 rail transportation workers in 1996, according to the Bureau of Labor Statistics, 25,000 of whom were conductors.

Starting Out

The method of becoming a conductor varies and is usually determined by a particular railroad company. Most often, applicants must start at entry-level jobs—such as messengers or janitors—and work their way up to foreman or conductor positions. After acquiring experience, they may be considered for the position of conductor. Some companies promote experienced personnel to conductor positions. At other companies, there is a specific sequence of jobs and training required before one becomes a conductor.

For example, one of the major railroads, Norfolk Southern, requires class and field training for freight service trainees to become conductor trainees. Field experience includes training with yard, local, and through freight crews. Completion of written exams is also required. Conductor trainees for Norfolk Southern undergo locomotive engineer training, including four weeks at a training facility and eight to twelve months of field training. The railroad lists the following duties for its conductor trainees: operate track switches, couple cars, and work on freight trains in yard operations and on the road.

Thus, the person interested in becoming a conductor must first seek employment at a lower-level job with a railroad company. Direct contact with unions and railroad companies is recommended for those interested in obtaining more information about an entry-level job. Such jobs serve as training for future conductors as they will be required to know all aspects of train operation.

Advancement

When conductors first begin their careers, they are seldom assigned regular full-time positions. Instead, they are put on a list called an "extra board" and are called in only when the railroad needs a substitute for a regular employee. On most railroads, conductors who are assigned to the extra board may work as brakers if there are not enough conductor runs available that month. The first form of promotion, then, is receiving a regular assignment as a conductor. Conductors who show promise and ability may eventually be promoted to managerial positions.

Earnings

As is the case with most rail occupations, the daily wage or hourly rate varies with the size of the railroad. Other factors that affect wages are the type of service, number of cars on the train, and the location of the train's run. For example, conductors receive extra pay on trains passing through mountainous regions. Usually, basic wages, as well as fringe benefits, for conductors are guaranteed by union contract.

The average annual wage for yard-freight conductors is $48,991, according to 1997 National Railroad Labor Conference figures. Local-freight conductors averaged $62,169 annually. Conductors generally belong to a union, so their rates of pay follow a specific schedule. In 1998, one major railroad paid conductor trainees $300 to $400 a week before taxes, or about $16,000 a year. Once they became full-fledged conductors, they earned $28,496 annually for the first year. After the fifth year of being a conductor, earnings increased to $35,672.

Conductors, like other railroad workers, receive a generous benefits package including health and life insurance, paid holidays and vacations, sick leave, and a pension plan. In addition to retirement plans sponsored by unions and railroads, conductors are eligible for Social Security and other government benefits.

Work Environment

Road conductors spend much of their time traveling and must be away from home on a constant basis. While assigned to the extra board, they usually have irregular hours. Once they receive a regular assignment, however, they may maintain a regular schedule and remain on a run for years. Although the basic workweek is eight hours for five days a week, days and nights are not considered different, and Sunday is treated as a workday. Along with other members of the train's crew, conductors work extra hours, including nights, weekends, and holidays, when travel is especially heavy. Mandatory rest periods are required for safety purposes. If a conductor is required to "lay over" while awaiting a train to return to the home terminal, he or she must pay for meals and other living expenses.

In addition to being a leader among other members of the train crew, the conductor also has the most direct and frequent contact with the public. The position can carry heavy responsibilities; it can also be very rewarding.

Outlook

Job opportunities are not promising for railroad conductors. Rail passenger services to many points have been discontinued. Although the volume of railroad freight business is expected to increase in the coming years, the use of mechanization, automation, and larger, faster trains is expected to cause a continued decline in the employment of rail transportation workers. Computers are now used to keep track of empty freight cars, match empty cars with the closest load, and dispatch trains. Also, new work rules that allow two- and three-person crews instead of the traditional five-person crews are becoming more widely used, and these factors combine to lessen the need for conductors and other crew workers.

Most job openings that arise in the future will be from a need to replace conductors who transfer to other kinds of work or who retire.

For More Information

For general information on the railroad industry, contact:

Association of American Railroads
50 F Street, NW
Washington, DC 20001
Tel: 202-639-2555
Web: http://www.aar.org

For information on the career of conductor, contact:

United Transportation Union
14600 Detroit Avenue
Cleveland, OH 44107-4250
Tel: 216-228-9400
Web: http://www.utu.org

Reservation and Ticket Agents

School Subjects

Business
English

Personal Skills

Communication/ideas
Helping/teaching

Work Environment

Primarily indoors
Primarily one location

Minimum Education Level

High school diploma

Salary Range

$11,000 to $25,000 to $39,000

Certification or Licensing

None available

Outlook

Decline

Overview

Reservation and ticket agents are employed by airlines, bus companies, railroads, and cruise lines to help customers in several ways. Reservation agents make and confirm reservations for passengers and use computers and manuals containing timetables, tariffs, and other information to plan the reservations and itinerary of travelers.

Ticket agents sell tickets at ticket counters in terminals or in ticket offices. They use computers and manuals containing scheduling, boarding, and rate information to plan routes and calculate ticket costs; make sure that seating is available; answer inquiries; check baggage and direct passengers to proper places for boarding; announce arrivals and departures; and assist passengers in boarding.

History

Since the earliest days of commercial passenger transportation by boat and overland stagecoach, someone has been responsible for making sure that space is available for all passengers and that everyone on board pays the fare. As transportation grew into a major industry over the years, the job of making reservations and selling tickets became a specialized occupation.

The airline industry experienced its first boom in the early 1930s. By the end of that decade, millions of people were flying each year. Since the introduction of passenger-carrying jet planes in 1958, the number of people traveling by air has multiplied many times over. Today the airlines handle more than 85 percent of all public travel within the United States and an even larger percentage of travel to cities overseas. These companies employ about three-fourths of all reservation and ticket agents.

A number of innovations have helped make the work of reservations and ticket agents easier and more efficient. The introduction of automated telephone services allows customers to be quickly transferred to a waiting agent. Computers have both simplified the agents' work and put more resources within their reach. Since the 1950s, many airlines have operated computerized scheduling and reservations systems, either individually or in partnership with other airlines. Until recently, these systems were not available to the general consumer. In the 1990s, however, the growth of the Internet and online services has permitted travelers to access scheduling and rate information, make reservations, and to purchase tickets without contacting an agent. The airlines have also begun to experiment with the so-called "electronic ticket," which they expect will eventually replace the traditional paper ticket. With these innovations, it is conceivable that one day there will be less need for reservation and ticketing agents. For the near future, however, these employees will still fill a vital role in the transportation industry.

The Job

Airline reservation agents are telephone-sales agents who work in large central offices run by the airline companies. Their primary job is to book and confirm reservations for passengers on scheduled airline flights. At the request of the customer or a ticket agent, they plan the itinerary and other arrangements. While many agents still use timetables, airline manuals, reference guides, and a tariff book, most of this work is performed using specialized computer programs.

After asking for the passenger's destination, desired travel time, and airport of departure, reservation agents type instructions into a computer and quickly obtain information on all flight schedules and seating availability. If the plane is full, the agent may suggest an alternate flight or check to see if space is available on another airline that flies to the same destination. Agents may even book seats on the competing airline, especially if their own airline can provide service on the return trip. Computers are used to make, confirm, change, and cancel reservations.

Reservation agents also answer telephone inquiries about such things as schedules, fares, arrival and departure times, and cities serviced by their airline. They may maintain an inventory of passenger space available so they can notify other personnel and ticket stations of changes and try to book all flights to capacity. Some reservation agents work in more specialized areas, handling calls from travel agents, or, with the airlines, bookings from members of the company's frequent flyer program. Agents working with international airlines must also be informed of any changes in visa regulations and other travel developments. This information is usually supplied by the senior reservation agent, who supervises and coordinates the activities of the other agents.

In the railroad industry, reservation clerks perform similar tasks. They receive requests for and assign seats or compartments to passengers, keep station agents and information clerks advised about available space, and communicate with reservation clerks in other towns.

Ticket agents for any transportation service—air, bus, rail, or ship—sell tickets to customers at terminals or at separate ticket offices. Like reservation agents, they book space for customers. In addition, they use computers to prepare and print tickets, calculate fares, and collect payment. At the terminals they check and tag luggage, direct passengers to the proper areas for boarding, keep records of passengers on each departure, and help with customer problems, such as lost baggage or missed connections. Airline ticket agents may have additional duties, such as paging arriving and departing passengers and finding hotel accommodations or new travel arrangements for passengers in the event of flight cancellations.

In airports, gate agents assign seats, issue boarding passes, make public address announcements of departures and arrivals, and help elderly or disabled passengers board the planes. They also make sure that the flight attendants have all the equipment they will need for their flight. They sometimes provide information to disembarking passengers about ground transportation, connecting flights, and local hotels.

The work of airline ticket agents is supervised by ticket sales supervisors, who may also perform the same duties as ticket agents. In airline central offices, ticketing clerks compile and record the information needed to assemble tickets that are mailed or otherwise sent to customers.

Regardless of where they work, reservation and transportation ticket agents must be knowledgeable about their companies' policies and procedures, as well as the standard procedures of their industry. They must be aware of the availability of special promotions and services and be able to answer any questions their customers may have.

Requirements

High School

Reservation and ticket agents are generally required to have at least a high school diploma. Job applicants should be able to type and have good communication and problem-solving skills. Because computers are being used more and more in this field, students should have at least a basic knowledge of computers and computer software. Previous experience working with the public is also helpful. Knowledge of foreign languages is also useful, especially for agents of companies providing international service.

Postsecondary Training

Some college is preferred, although it is not considered essential. (Some junior colleges offer courses specifically designed for students wanting to become ticket agents.) New reservation agents are given about a month of classroom instruction. They are taught to read schedules, calculate fares, and plan itineraries. They learn how to use the computer to get information and reserve space. They also learn about company policies and government regulations that apply to the industry.

Ticket agents receive about one week of classroom instruction. They learn how to read tickets and schedules, assign seats, and tag baggage. This is followed by one week of on-the-job training, working alongside an experienced agent. After mastering the simpler tasks, the new ticket agents are trained to reserve space, make out tickets, and handle the boarding gate.

Other Requirements

Because reservation and ticket agents are in constant contact with the public, a well-groomed, professional appearance, a clear and pleasant speaking voice, and a friendly personality are important qualities. Agents need to be tactful in keeping telephone time to a minimum without alienating their customers. In addition, agents must enjoy working with people, have a good memory, and be able to maintain their composure when working with harried or unhappy travelers. Reservation and ticket agents form a large part of the public image of their company.

Many agents belong to such labor unions as the Air Line Employees Association; the Transport Workers Union of America; the Transportation Communications International Union; and the International Brotherhood of Teamsters, Chauffeurs, Warehousemen and Helpers of America.

Exploring

High school students may wish to apply for part-time or summer work with transportation companies in their central offices or at terminals. A school counselor can try to arrange an informational interview with an experienced reservation and transportation ticket agent. This interview may provide more information on the daily activities of such individuals. Even if the duties are only vaguely related, the students will at least have the opportunity to become familiar with transportation operations.

Employers

The commercial airlines are the main employers of reservation and ticket agents. However, other transportation companies—rail, ship, and bus, primarily—also require their services.

Starting Out

College placement services may be able to provide information or job listings for those students entering this field. High school students can find part-time or summer work in these or related jobs. Job applicants may also apply directly to the personnel or employment offices of the transportation companies for current information about job openings, requirements, and possible training programs. Many unions also provide lists of job openings.

Advancement

With experience and a good work record, some reservation and ticket agents can be promoted to supervisory positions. A few may become city and district sales managers for ticket offices. Beyond this, opportunities for advancement are limited. However, achieving seniority with a company may give the agent the first choice of shifts and available overtime.

Earnings

Starting salaries for airline reservation agents vary widely depending on the airline, although most fall between $11,000 and $19,000 per year. Ticket agents and reservation agents overall earn between $12,000 and $40,000 per year, with supervisors earning the top salaries. In 1995, the average weekly wage for reservation agents was $467, while ticket agents averaged $511 per week. In the railroad industry, Amtrak agents earned between $22,000 and $30,000. Bus companies tended to pay lower wages to their agents. Most agents can earn overtime pay; many employers also pay extra for night work. Benefits vary according to the place of work, the number of years worked, and union membership, although most agents receive vacation and sick pay, health insurance, and retirement plans. Agents, especially when employed by the airlines, often receive free or reduced-fare transportation for themselves and their families.

Work Environment

Reservation agents typically work in cubicles with their own computer terminals and telephone headsets. Reservation and ticket agents generally work 40 hours a week. These agents speak all day on the telephone, while using their computers. Their telephone conversations and computer activity may be monitored and recorded by their supervisors. They might also be required to achieve sales or reservations quotas. The work is very hectic during holidays and other busy periods or when special promotions and discounts are being offered. At these and other times, such as periods of severe weather, passengers may become difficult. Such situations can make the job stressful. Nevertheless, agents must maintain their composure and a pleasant manner when speaking with customers.

Ticket agents work in airports and train and bus stations, which can be busy and noisy. These agents stand most of the day and often lift heavy objects such as luggage and packages. During holidays and busy times, their work can become extremely hectic as they process long lines of waiting customers. Storms and other factors may delay or even cancel flights, trains, and bus services, and at these times the agent may be confronted with upset passengers. The agent must be able to maintain his or her composure at all times.

Outlook

Three out of four of the more than 100,000 reservation and transportation ticket agents work for the airlines. However, the position is likely to decline through the year 2006. Technology is changing the way consumers purchase tickets. "Ticketless" travel, or automated reservations ticketing, is reducing the need for ticket agents. Most airports have kiosks that allow passengers to reserve and purchase tickets themselves. Passengers can also access information about fares and flight times on the Internet, where they can make reservations and purchase tickets. For security reasons, all of these services cannot be fully automated, so reservation and transportation ticket agents will not be phased out.

Most openings will occur as experienced agents transfer to other occupations or retire. Competition, however, is heavy because of the glamour of working for an airline and because of the attractive travel benefits. Competition is also keen because of the relatively low turnover rate among these workers and the fact that the supply of applicants greatly exceeds the demand. Overall, the transportation industry will remain heavily dependent on the state of the economy.

For More Information

For information on education, internship, scholarship, or certification in travel and tourism, contact:

National Tourism Foundation
546 East Main Street
PO Box 3071
Lexington, KY 40596-3071
Tel: 800-682-8886 or 606-226-4251
Web: http://www.ntaonline.com

Route Drivers

School Subjects

Business
Computer science
Technical/Shop

Personal Skills

Following instructions

Work Environment

Indoors and outdoors
Primarily multiple locations

Minimum Education Level

High school diploma
Apprenticeship

Salary Range

$12,000 to $20,000 to $25,000+

Certification or Licensing

Required by all states

Outlook

Little change or more slowly than the average

Overview

Route drivers, also known as *route-sales drivers* or *driver-sales workers,* drive trucks over established routes and deliver products such as milk, baked goods, soft drinks, laundry, dry cleaning, and ice cream to regular customers. What a driver delivers depends on his or her employer's products. Customers may be retail establishments, the general public, or both. Drivers usually collect payments from customers and attempt to interest them in new products or services offered by the company.

Route drivers may use their own trucks and operate as independent businesspersons. Otherwise, drivers work for businesses that provide the vehicles. Most route drivers work for companies based in large urban areas. Over 500,000 route drivers are employed in the United States.

History

In the United States, there have always been individuals who earned their livelihoods by selling materials and merchandise from door to door. The peddler is probably the oldest sales worker in the United States. By going from door to door, with their goods loaded in a horse-drawn cart, peddlers established wide commercial networks and were able to provide a supply of goods to remote areas of the United States.

To some extent, the Yankee peddler of colonial times has been replaced by the route-sales drivers. Industries have delegated the responsibilities of merchandising and marketing to their own sales departments and other employees. Route drivers not only deliver the company's products, but must also be skilled in the art of sales, which the peddler first developed.

Over the years, the products sold by route drivers and the manner in which they are delivered have been influenced by important developments in society. For example, in the early 20th century, automobiles and trucks replaced horse-drawn carts as transportation for sales workers. Also, construction of new and better roads made it possible for one driver to cover more territory and serve more people.

A route driver interacted with people all day as he or she stopped at several businesses and residences to pick up and deliver parcels. As industry advanced, new products and new merchandising methods continued to change the demands placed on route drivers. For example, as convenience stores became more numerous and people increasingly relied on them for everyday items, fewer people had milk and baked goods delivered to their homes. The growth of mail-order catalog houses as well as the trend of stores buying directly from suppliers, further decreased the number of positions open for route drivers.

Today, route drivers are more specialized than their predecessors. Instead of selling many things to a small number of people, as did the all-purpose peddler, they sell fewer products and services to a larger number of people.

The items sold and customer base aren't the only things that have changed. For many sales route drivers, the route map, sales slips, and paper receipts have all been automated. Although many route drivers still use the paper-based forms, many route drivers have electronic maps, computerized inventory takers, and electronic hand-held receipt/signature machines.

The Job

Route drivers usually drive panel or light trucks. They not only deliver, but also sell products that range from dry-cleaning services to pastries. Drivers' duties vary with the kinds of items or services they sell, the size of the company they work for, and the kind of route they service.

Route drivers who sell, collect, or deliver to retail establishments are known as wholesale route drivers, and those who provide similar services directly to the public are known as retail route drivers. Retail route drivers make five to ten times more deliveries per day than wholesale route drivers.

The majority of route drivers are employed by dairies, bakeries, and laundry and dry-cleaning plants located in large cities. These men and women provide bakery, milk, dry cleaning, laundry, newspapers, and other goods and services that people use every day.

The particular duties of route drivers vary according to the industry in which they are employed, the policies of their particular company, and how strongly their sales responsibilities are emphasized. Route drivers may load or supervise the loading of their delivery truck, deliver previously ordered material to stops on assigned routes, obtain new orders, collect payments, and keep records of the transactions. From time to time, drivers solicit the business of new stores on their route.

After completing the day's deliveries, route drivers turn in the payments they have collected. Then route drivers order items for the next day that they think customers are likely to buy, based primarily on what products have been selling well, the weather, time of year, and any discussions they may have had with customers.

Wholesale bakery route drivers, for example, deliver and arrange bread, cakes, rolls, and other baked goods on display racks in grocery stores. By paying close attention to the items that are selling well and those that are just sitting on the shelves, they estimate the amount and variety of baked goods that will be sold. A driver may recommend changes in a store's order or may encourage the manager to stock new bakery products.

Newspaper-delivery drivers deliver newspapers and magazines to dealers and vending machines; newspaper carriers deliver them directly to subscribers. Both types of workers collect money and keep records. *Lunch-truck drivers* sell sandwiches, box lunches, drinks, and similar items to factory and office workers, students, and people attending outdoor events. *Coin collectors* collect and distribute coins to vending machines.

Requirements

High School

Employers prefer that potential route drivers be high school graduates. Interested high school students should take courses in sales, public speaking, driver training, mechanics, bookkeeping, and business arithmetic. Courses in merchandising and retailing are also helpful.

Postsecondary Training

College and university level training is not necessary for route sales drivers, although classes in sales and business may give you the advantage over others applying for these positions.

Certification or Licensing

In most states, drivers must qualify for a commercial driver's license. State motor vehicle departments can provide information on how to qualify for this license. An attractive candidate will also know the location of streets in certain sections of an urban area and be able to use maps. Route drivers must also be excellent drivers. For insurance reasons, employers generally prefer to hire drivers who are at least 25 years of age and have an impeccable driving record.

Other Requirements

Drivers work without direct supervision and must be extremely responsible individuals. Drivers must have orderly work habits because they prepare instructions for other workers who are to fill orders. Bookkeeping skills and an eye for detail helps a driver keep accurate records of the payments his or her customers must make.

Bruce Lane, a delivery route driver from California, comments on the importance of being a responsible worker, "Generally, you are working alone, with little or no supervision or guidance. You must assume the responsibility for making sure the job gets done every day."

The success of route drivers depends on how well they keep their present customers happy and the number of new customers they enlist. To fulfill these requirements, route drivers must have self-confidence, initiative, and tact. Above all, they must be honest and have personal integrity. Route drivers should enjoy meeting a wide variety of people and be able to interact with them comfortably, especially those route drivers who work directly with the public. They must also help customers who have complaints about the products or services they receive. Handling customer complaints well can mean the difference between keeping and losing a client. In addition, a driver's effectiveness as a salesperson is increased if he or she is neat in appearance and pleasant in manner. Most route drivers wear uniforms. In some cases, companies pay for these uniforms and for their cleaning.

Exploring

If you are a high school student and interested in this career, you may want to obtain a part-time or summer job as a route driver's helper, in order to see if a career as a route driver is right for you. You can also visit laundries, bakeries, dry-cleaning plants, and other establishments to observe route drivers preparing their trucks for deliveries. Professional route drivers can also answer questions about job responsibilities.

Newspaper delivery jobs are a good first step to learning the daily routine of a route driver. Although sales isn't usually a part of this type of delivery work, customer service, responsibility for cargo, and timeliness are paramount. The Internet also provides a forum for discussing a career as a route driver. The site for the trucking news group is news.misc.transport.trucking. The American Trucking Associations has a World Wide Web site at http://www.truckline.com.

Employers

Route drivers are employed by companies of all kinds. Any business that needs to get their product from the warehouse, plant, or store and into the hands of their customers uses delivery drivers to make that happen. Some employers simply need the product delivered, such as newspaper publishers, package delivery services, and florists; other employers need the product delivered and new sales generated, such as restaurant equipment companies, cleaning supply companies, and so on. Route driver positions are available across the country, although more positions are usually found in the larger cities.

Starting Out

Route drivers can attain their positions in several ways. Some begin in a job as a retail sales worker or other type of salesperson. Others start out as a route driver's helper upon graduation from high school or during summer vacations and accept positions as route drivers when openings develop. Sales route-driver helpers assist the route driver in various ways, such as loading and unloading the truck; carrying goods from the truck to the customer's office, store, or house; and driving. Still others wait for the proper opportunity and look for jobs, as dockworkers or other positions, in plants that employ route drivers.

If you are interested in being an independent route driver, Bruce suggests preparing yourself with the correct tools; "When you take a delivery job, you are basically going into business for yourself. You need to prepare by getting the right vehicle and insurance. Access to a second vehicle as backup is a necessity."

Many large companies have on-the-job training programs. Employees who look like good candidates for route driver jobs are trained to ensure that they are knowledgeable of the products they will sell. A company may also assign new drivers to work a route with an experienced driver or supervisor for a brief period of time.

Advancement

Many route drivers look forward to moving into positions as sales supervisors and route supervisors, but these positions are relatively scarce. Route sales-delivery driver supervisors supervise and coordinate the work of route drivers. They plan routes and schedules, collect cash receipts, handle customer complaints, keep records, and solicit new business.

Most retail route drivers advance by taking positions as wholesale route drivers because higher salaries usually come with wholesale routes. Other route drivers use the experience they have gained on their routes to take sales positions in other fields in which earnings are higher. Also, route drivers that have gained driving experience may aspire to become long-distance truck drivers.

Earnings

Most route drivers work for a salary plus a commission on their sales. Wholesale route drivers generally make more money than retail route drivers because they sell items in large quantities and therefore get larger commissions. The earnings of route drivers are related to their effectiveness as persuasive salespeople. Wages also differ depending on the region in which a route driver works and the kind of product they deliver. On average, route drivers earn between $12,000 and $25,000 annually. Some route drivers may contract with an organization, such as a newspaper publisher, and then be paid by the customers on a monthly basis.

Route drivers are a highly unionized group within the trucking industry. The largest number of route drivers belong to the International Brotherhood of Teamsters, Chauffeurs, Warehousemen, and Helpers of America. Other route drivers are members of the unions representing plant workers or their employers. Generally, union drivers receive higher wages than nonunion drivers.

Route drivers enjoy various fringe benefits. Some have paid vacations ranging from one to four weeks, and some have paid holidays. Some route drivers are provided medical benefits and are covered by pension plans.

Work Environment

There are great differences in the number of hours route drivers work. Some route drivers work more than 60 hours a week; others work only 30 hours. The number of hours that route drivers work is determined by a number of factors, including the season of the year, the ambition of the individual route driver, union regulations, and the nature of the route. Some route drivers, such as those delivering milk or newspapers, have to work unusual hours, typically beginning their routes at 4:00 or 5:00 AM. Bruce knows that scenario well; "In most cases you are working at night, so the traffic and parking hassles are minimum, but some people are afraid to be out alone in the dark. Also, most routes are two to four hours per day, and because of the hours involved it is difficult to work the route around another full-time job."

Retail route drivers have to make deliveries in all kinds of weather and do a good deal of lifting, carrying, and climbing. Working indoors and outdoors is an attractive benefit of being a route driver. This means that route drivers get to enjoy beautiful weather, as well as suffer through extreme heat and cold. Improvements in technology have made the cabs of trucks much more comfortable, but on the hottest of summer days this is of little solace.

Traffic conditions can also make driving a truck in a major urban center rather stressful. Excellent driving skills and the ability to keep calm is essential when navigating congested streets and narrow alleys. Route drivers should also be aware of road restrictions. Some roads have size and weight limitations, while others have commercial vehicle restrictions. Some communities have barred vehicles such as ice cream trucks because of the potential danger of a child running into the road.

Despite these conditions, many drivers find the opportunity to work independently and the challenge of selling essential products and services very satisfying.

Outlook

According to the U.S. Bureau of Labor Statistics, more than 500,000 sales route drivers are employed in the United States. The country has experienced a decline in the number of retail route drivers since 1940, due to a number of factors. During World War II, the shortage of workers and gasoline made it necessary to cut sharply the number of home deliveries of products. Delivery was never fully resumed after the war. Also, many people now have large refrigerators and home freezers, which reduces the need for fresh bakery and dairy products to be delivered at homes daily.

A number of large companies have developed so many products that one route driver cannot handle all of them. As a result, many wholesale route drivers have been replaced by sales workers. These sales workers take orders, which are later delivered by truck drivers. This is especially true in areas where large supermarkets have replaced small grocery stores. The development of new products, however, has increased the need for wholesale route drivers to introduce these products in food stores throughout the country.

These changes may have run their course, and the number of route drivers is expected to change little in the foreseeable future. Because of retirements, deaths, and transfers, there will continue to be a need for retail route drivers each year. In addition, the population of the nation continues to move toward the suburbs, where there is expected to be an increased need for these services.

For More Information

To learn more about the union most sales route drivers join, contact:

International Brotherhood of Teamsters, Chauffeurs, Warehousemen, and Helpers of America
25 Louisiana Avenue, NW
Washington, DC 20001
Tel: 202-624-6800
Web: http://www.teamster.org/

For general information about route driving, contact:

American Trucking Associations
Office of Public Affairs
2200 Mill Road
Alexandria, VA 22314-4677
Tel: 703-838-1700
Web: http://www.truckline.com

Signal Mechanics

School Subjects
Computer science
Technical/Shop

Personal Skills
Mechanical/manipulative
Technical/scientific

Work Environment
Primarily outdoors
Primarily multiple locations

Minimum Education Level
Apprenticeship

Salary Range
$27,500 to $33,456 to $37,428

Certification or Licensing
None available

Outlook
Little change or more slowly than the average

Overview

Signal mechanics or *signal maintainers* are railroad employees who install, repair, and maintain the signals, signal equipment, and gate crossings that are part of the traffic control and communications systems along railroad tracks. They keep both electrical and mechanical components of signaling devices in good operating order by routinely inspecting and testing lights, circuits and wiring, crossing gates, and detection devices.

History

Railroad signals were developed to let train crews know about conditions on the track ahead of them. Signaling systems became necessary in the 19th century when early steam-driven trains began to operate so fast that they presented the danger of collision with one another. Smooth rails and wheels allowed trains to carry heavy loads easily and efficiently, but as speeds and load weights increased, trains needed longer stopping distances. Train crews had to be sure that they were not headed toward another train coming in the opposite direction on the same track, and they had to maintain a safe distance between trains moving in the same direction.

The first attempt to avoid accidents was the adoption of a timetable system. This system was based on running trains on timed schedules, so that there was always a space between them. However, if a train broke down, the next train's crew had to be informed somehow so that it could react appropriately. In 1837, on a rail line in England, a telegraph system was introduced in which signals were sent on telegraph wires between stations up and down the tracks. The track was divided into blocks, or sections, with a signalman responsible for each block. As trains passed through the blocks, one signalman telegraphed messages to the next block, allowing the next signalman to decide whether it was safe for the train to proceed through that block.

In 1841, a system was devised for communicating with train operators using a mechanical version of semaphore arm signals. At night, when the signal flags could not be seen, a light source was used, with different colored lenses that were rotated in front of it. In time, various codes and rules were developed so that train crews could be kept informed about track conditions ahead as they moved from block to block.

As rail traffic increased, many refinements in signaling systems reduced the chance of human error and helped make train traffic run more smoothly. In 1872, an automatic block system was introduced in which the track itself was part of an electrical circuit, and various signals were activated when the train passed over the track. A modern version of this invention is the moving block system, in which a kind of zone is electronically maintained around a train, and the speed of nearby trains is regulated automatically. Today, traffic control in rail systems is largely centralized and computerized. Many trains and cars can be monitored at one time, and signals and switches can be operated remotely to manage the system with maximum safety and efficiency.

In order for these sophisticated controls to be effective, railroad signals and signaling equipment must function properly. Signal mechanics are the workers who are responsible for making sure that this vital equipment is working as it is intended.

The Job

Signal mechanics install, maintain, and repair signal equipment. Today's signal equipment includes computerized and electronic equipment detection devices and electronic grade crossing protection. To install signals, workers travel with road crews to designated areas. They place electrical wires, create circuits, and construct railway-highway crossing signals, such as flashers and gates. When signal mechanics install new signals or signal equipment, they or other crew members may have to dig holes and pour concrete foundations for the new equipment, or they may install precast concrete foundations. Because railroad signal systems are sometimes installed in the same areas as underground fiber optic cables, signal mechanics must be familiar with marking systems and take great care in digging.

Signal mechanics who perform routine maintenance are generally responsible for a specified length of track. They are often part of a team of several signal mechanics, called a signal construction gang. They drive a truck along the track route, stopping to inspect and test crossings, signal lights, interlock equipment, and detection devices. When servicing battery-operated equipment, they check batteries, refilling them with water or replacing them with fresh ones if necessary. They use standard electrical testing devices to check signal circuits and wiring connections, and they replace any defective wiring, burned-out light bulbs, or broken colored lenses on light signals. They clean the lenses with a cloth and cleaning solution and lubricate moving parts on swinging signal arms and crossing gates. They tighten loose bolts, and open and close crossing gates to verify that the circuits and connections in the gates are working.

Signal mechanics are often required to travel long distances as repairs are needed. Many are assigned to a large region by their employer, such as the entire Midwest, or may even be on call to work anywhere in the nation. Generally, employees are responsible for providing their own transportation from their home to the work location. The railroad company pays the cost of hotel rooms and provides a meal allowance. When signal mechanics are required to travel, their work week may begin on Sunday, when they travel to the work site so they can start early Monday. The work week may then include four 10-hour days, or longer, depending on the urgency of completing the job.

Sometimes signal mechanics are dispatched to perform repairs at specific locations along the track in response to reports from other rail workers about damaged or malfunctioning equipment. In these cases, the worker analyzes the problem, repairs it, and checks to make sure that the equipment is functioning properly.

Signal mechanics also compile written reports that detail their inspection and repair activities, noting the mileage of the track that they have traveled and the locations where they have done work.

Requirements

High School

Proven mechanical aptitude is very desirable, and a firm knowledge of electricity is a must. Because of the change in technology in signaling in the railroad industry, railroads are requiring new job applicants to pass written tests that include AC/DC electronics. Therefore, high school courses in electrical shop and electronics would provide a good background for signal mechanics. Technical training in computers is also very helpful.

Postsecondary Training

Signal mechanics must have at least a high school diploma, although some railroads have gone so far as to require applicants to have college degrees in electronics or electrical engineering. Other railroads will consider applicants who have military experience in electronics, or who possess a two-year degree in electronics from a technical school.

Workers are usually trained both on the job and in the classroom. Some of the biggest railroads have their own schools; the smaller ones often contract to send their employees to those schools. For example, Norfolk Southern sends its signal trainees to its training center in McDonough, Georgia, during which they are paid a training wage, and lodging and meals are paid for during the one-week training course.

Subjects studied in the classroom include electrical and electronics theory; mathematics; signal apparatus, protection devices, and circuits; federal railroad administration policies; and procedures related to signaling.

On the job, beginners often start out in helper positions, doing simple tasks requiring little special skill. Helpers work under the supervision of experienced signal mechanics. Later, they may become assistants and signal maintainers, based on their seniority and how much they have learned.

Other Requirements

Skilled workers in signal departments usually do not need great strength or stamina, although they may have to be active throughout the day, perhaps climbing poles or hand digging with shovels and picks. Signal mechanics need to be able to climb, stoop, kneel, crouch, and reach, and they should also be agile, with a good sense of balance. Good vision, normal hearing, and depth perception are important. Finally, alertness and quick reflexes are needed for working in potentially dangerous circumstances on ladders, near high-voltage lines, and on moving equipment.

Most signal mechanics who work for the larger railroads are required to belong to a union—usually the Brotherhood of Railroad Signalmen. Those who work for the smaller railroads are typically nonunionized.

Exploring

A field trip to a rail yard can give a student a firsthand idea of the work done in this occupation. For a closer view, it may be possible to talk with a railroad employee who is involved in maintaining communications or control equipment. Professional journals, such as the *Signalman's Journal,* published by the Brotherhood of Railroad Signalmen, can provide useful information about the career of signal mechanics.

Employers

Signal mechanics may be employed by passenger lines or freight lines. They may work for one of the major railroads, such as Burlington Northern Santa Fe, Norfolk Southern, CSX, or Atchison-Topeka-Santa Fe, or they may work for one of the 500 smaller short-line railroads across the country. Many of the passenger lines today are commuter lines located near large metropolitan areas. Signal mechanics who work for freight lines may work in a rural or an urban area and travel more extensively than the shorter, daily commuter routes passenger railroad conductors make.

Starting Out

Prospective signal mechanics can contact the personnel offices of railroad companies for information about job opportunities. Another possibility is to check with the local, state, or national office of the Brotherhood of Railroad Signalmen. Because signal mechanic positions are often union positions, they follow structured hiring procedures, such as specific times of the year when applications are accepted. Norfolk Southern holds hiring/recruiting sessions. Applications are not sent out for union positions; rather recruiting sessions are advertised in local newspapers, state job services, and schools. At recruiting sessions, supervisors explain the positions open, answer questions, and oversee the application process. Some applicants may be selected for evaluations, which will be used to help determine who is hired.

Advancement

Workers generally advance from helper positions to become assistant signal mechanics, and from there to positions as signal maintainers. Other advanced positions include signal shop foremen and signal inspectors. These promotions, which are related to workers' seniority, sometimes take a number of years to achieve. Experienced signal mechanics can advance to such supervisory positions as gang foremen or leaders of work crews, directing and coordinating the activities of other signal mechanics. At one railroad, Norfolk Southern, signal mechanics are designated as assistant signal persons after qualifying as trainees. After completing two phases of training and based on seniority, assistant signal persons can bid for promotion to a signal maintainer position with territorial maintenance responsibilities.

Earnings

Currently, signal mechanics and signal maintainers earn almost $37,000 annually. Signal helpers and signal maintainer helpers earn about $27,500. According to the agreement between the Brotherhood of Railroad Signalmen and one major railroad, signal shop foremen earn the highest salary, $37,428 per year, followed by signal gang foremen at $34,848 and assistant signal foremen, who earn $33,456. These rates are based on 213 hours of work per month, which generally means workers work six-day weeks, and do not include overtime.

Workers receive extra pay for overtime work. In addition to regular earnings, they receive fringe benefits such as employer contributions to health insurance and retirement plans, paid vacation days, and travel passes.

Work Environment

Signal department workers do their work outdoors in a variety of weather conditions, sometimes at night. Some workers are regularly scheduled to be on call for emergency repairs.

In some cases, signal mechanics must lift, carry, and push or pull somewhat heavy objects. They may also be required to stoop, squat, climb, and crawl into small spaces. Mechanics must use caution on the job to avoid hazards such as falling from ladders or signal towers, being hit by falling objects, and electric shock.

There is variety in the kinds of signals a mechanic works on, and variety in the location of the work, so the job is rarely boring. In addition, workers in this field can take pride in the importance of their responsibilities, since railroad travel is heavily dependent upon the proper functioning of signals.

Outlook

In the coming years, the number of signal mechanics who install signal equipment is not expected to grow; however, the number of signal maintainers, who test the signaling and communications equipment may increase, due to the more complex circuitry involved in the signaling systems. Relatively few additional job openings will develop, and they will mostly occur when experienced workers transfer to other fields or leave the workforce altogether.

For More Information

For general information on the railroad industry, contact:

Association of American Railroads
50 F Street, NW
Washington, DC 20001
Tel: 202-639-2100
Web: http://www.aar.org

For information on the career of railroad signal mechanic, contact:

Brotherhood of Railroad Signalmen
601 West Golf Road, Box U
Mount Prospect, IL 60056
Tel: 847-439-3732
Web: http://www.brs.org

Stevedores

School Subjects

Mathematics
Physical education

Personal Skills

Following instructions
Mechanical/manipulative

Work Environment

Primarily outdoors
Primarily multiple locations

Minimum Education Level

High school diploma

Salary Range

$45,000 to $60,000 to $100,000

Certification or Licensing

None available

Outlook

Little change or more slowly than the average

Overview

Stevedores, commonly known as *longshore workers* or *dockworkers,* handle cargo at ports, often using materials-handling machinery and gear. They load and unload ships at docks and transfer cargo to and from storage areas or other transports, such as trucks and barges. Members of the water transportation industry, stevedores are employed at ports all over the United States. The concentration of jobs is at the large ports on the coasts, and most of the positions are held by experienced, skilled workers.

History

There have been stevedoring workers in North America since colonial times. Long ago, when a sailing vessel arrived at the docks of a settlement, criers would go up and down the nearby streets summoning workers with a call like "Men along the shore!" Stevedores, or longshore workers, came quickly in hopes of a chance to make some extra cash by helping to unload the ship's cargo. Often, these longshore workers lived in town near the port and worked other occupations. Ships arrived too infrequently for them to make a living at the docks. But as the volume of shipping increased, a group of workers developed who were always available at the docks for loading and unloading activities.

Ship owners usually wanted to have cargos moved through ports as soon as possible. They preferred to pick temporary workers from a large labor pool at the time there was work to be done. However, this practice produced unfavorable wages, hours, and working conditions for many workers. In the 19th century, longshore workers were among the first groups of American workers to organize labor unions to force improvements in working conditions.

In ancient times, a ship's cargo was handled in single "man-loads." Grain, a common item of cargo, was packed in sacks that could be carried on and off the ship on a man's shoulders. As methods progressed, the ship's rigging became used for hoisting cargo. The first cargo to need a special type of handling was fuel, which used to be transported in barrels. As the volume of fuel increased, barrels became inadequate. Since the late 19th century, oil products have been shipped in bulk, with no packaging, pumped directly into the hull cells of tankers.

Cargo handling has thus depended on the type of cargo shipped. Vehicles are simply rolled on and off; dry bulk like coal and grain is often poured into cargo holds. In the first part of the 20th century, longshore work slowly became mechanized, relying less on human labor and more on machines. Since the 1960s, containerization of cargos has been a major factor in ocean shipping. This method of transporting goods involves putting freight into large sealed boxes of standard sizes, sometimes fitted as truck trailers. The containers, which can be carried on ships that are specially built to hold them, are easily and quickly moved on and off ships at ports, thus keeping the cost of transport well below that for uncontainerized cargo. Such changes have greatly reduced the demand for stevedoring workers to do manual loading and unloading.

This can be considered a historic time for women's opportunities in these occupations. In the late 20th century, more longshore workers than ever before were women. Sexual discrimination lawsuits are forcing companies to hire more females. In California, for example, where there are many docks because of the state's long coastline, there were no women dockworkers until 1974. Now hundreds of women hold longshore positions at ports along the California coast.

The Job

Stevedores perform tasks involved in transferring cargo to and from the holds of ships and around the dock area. They may operate power winches or cranes to move items such as automobiles, crates, scrap metal, and steel beams, using hooks, magnets, or slings. They may operate grain trimmers (equipment that moves bulk grain through a spout and into the hatch of receiving containers). Stevedores may drive trucks along the dock or aboard ships to transfer items such as lumber and crates to within reach of winches. They may drive tractors to move loaded trailers from storage areas to dockside. They may load and unload liquid cargos, such as vegetable oils, molasses, or chemicals, by fastening hose lines to cargo tanks. Stevedores also do other manual tasks such as lashing cargo in place aboard ships, attaching lifting devices to winches, and signaling to other workers to raise or lower cargo. They may direct other dockworkers in moving cargo by hand or with handtrucks or in securing cargo inside the holds of ships.

Some stevedoring workers perform just one category of specialized tasks. For example, *boat loaders* may load liquid chemical and fuel cargos such as petroleum, gasoline, heating oil, and sulfuric acid by connecting and disconnecting hose couplings. At each stage in the process, they make sure various conditions are safe. Other boat loaders tend winches and loading chutes to load iron ore onto boats and barges. Winch drivers operate steam or electric winches to move various kinds of cargo in and out of a ship's hold. They may alternate jobs with hatch tenders, who signal to winch drivers when the cargo is secured and ready for transfer. *Gear repairers* fix gear that is used in lifting cargo and install appropriate equipment depending on the current cargo-handling needs on a particular vessel. Among the many other workers in the dock area are *drivers,* who drive rolling stock (including forklifts, trucks, and mobile cranes), and *carpenters,* who repair pallets and construct braces and other structures to protect cargo in holds or on deck.

Headers or *gang bosses* supervise stevedores. They assign specific duties and explain how the cargo should be handled and secured and how the hoisting equipment should be set up. They may estimate the amount of extra materials that will be needed to brace and protect the cargo, such as paper or lumber.

Stevedoring superintendents are responsible for coordinating and directing the loading and unloading of cargo. Before loading begins, they study the layout of the ship and the bill of lading to determine where to stow cargo and in what order. Freight that must come out first is usually the last to be loaded. Stevedoring superintendents estimate the time and number of workers they need for the job and give orders for hiring. They make sure that the available equipment is appropriate for the cargo load, and they may direct workers who are handling special materials, such as explosives. Stevedoring superintendents prepare reports on their operations and may make up bills, all the while keeping in touch with the company representatives from whom they get their directions.

Pier superintendents manage business operations at freight terminals. They determine what cargo various vessels will be carrying and notify stevedoring superintendents to plan to have workers and dock space available for loading and unloading activities. They compute costs; oversee purchasing of cargo handling equipment and hiring of trucks, tractors, and railroad cars; and make sure that the terminal facilities and the company's equipment are properly maintained.

Shipping operations require individuals who have good recordkeeping and accounting skills as well. Workers who do these tasks include *shipping clerks,* who maintain information on all incoming and outgoing cargo, such as its quantity and condition, identification marks, and container size. *Location workers* keep track of where cargo is located on piers. *Delivery clerks* and *receiving clerks* keep records on the loading and discharging of vessels and on transferring cargo to and from truckers. *Timekeepers* record the work time of all workers on the pier for billing and payroll purposes.

Requirements

High School

If you think you might be interested in becoming a stevedore, you should take classes in mathematics and English as well as shop and physical education to help prepare you for the different aspects of the workload.

Postsecondary Training

Often, no special preparation is needed for this kind of work because many stevedores learn what they need to know, such as equipment operations, on the job. However, experience operating similar equipment is likely to be an advantage to any applicant and may result in more rapid advancement.

Workers in some positions need clerical or technical skills that can be learned in high school or vocational school. For administrative occupations, college-level training or experience as a ship's officer is often desirable.

Supervisory personnel generally need an understanding of the whole process of loading and unloading a vessel. They must be able to deal with a labor force that may include inexperienced workers and that changes in number from day to day.

Many stevedoring jobs are open only to union workers. Unions to which stevedores belong are the International Longshoremen's Association and the International Longshoremen's and Warehousemen's Union. In some ports, jobs are allocated based on seniority, so newcomers may be left with the least desirable jobs.

Other Requirements

Stevedores who work on the docks need to be agile and physically fit. Their work may be strenuous, sometimes requiring lifting weights of up to 50 pounds. Good eyesight and dexterity are essential. Some jobs can be adapted to some extent for workers with disabilities. Stevedores may work in situations that are potentially dangerous, so they must be able to think clearly and quickly and be able to follow orders. Because longshore work is a team effort, stevedores must work well with others.

Exploring

To find out more about stevedoring occupations, contact the offices of the longshore workers' union in your area. Union representatives can provide you with information about the likely conditions and prospects for local jobs, as well as answer questions and provide an insider's view of the field. Students in coastal areas have an advantage over others because they can visit ports and ask questions about what is involved in being a dockworker.

Employers

Stevedores are employed at all U.S. ports. The bulk of jobs are concentrated on the coasts, and larger companies employ greater numbers of longshore workers. Usually, you must be a union member to secure a position with one of the larger companies.

Starting Out

To find a job as a stevedore, you should contact the local union offices or shipping companies to find out whether workers are being hired. Those who would like eventually to work in an administrative position, such as pier superintendent, should consider entering one of the maritime academies (schools that train officers and crew for merchant vessels). Another possibility for people interested in administrative work is to enter a training program conducted by a port authority, which is an organization at a port that controls harbor activities.

Advancement

Dockworkers may start out doing basic labor, such as loading trucks or following instructions to load cargo in holds. Later, if they prove to be responsible and reliable, they may learn how to operate equipment such as winches or forklifts. In general, this kind of advancement depends on the need for workers to do particular tasks as well as the individual's abilities. Those who demonstrate strong abilities, leadership, and judgment may have an opportunity to become gang bosses and supervise a crew of other workers. Advancement into administrative positions may require additional formal education.

Earnings

Wages for stevedores on the East Coast average around $60,000 per year, with supervisory and administrative workers averaging more. Experienced workers on the West Coast can earn $85,000 to $100,000 per year. Minimum wages can be negotiated by unions; in 1994, the International Longshoremen's Association's union contract called for a minimum wage of $22 per hour. Stevedores receive extra pay for handling certain difficult or dangerous cargoes and for working overtime, nights, or holidays. In addition to earnings, full-time workers usually receive good benefits packages that may include pension plans, paid holiday and vacation days, and health insurance.

One type of benefit plan, Guaranteed Annual Income (GAI), a program that pays dockworkers even when they are not working, is being eliminated by many ports. When work is scarce, the GAI plan can be expensive for companies. Thus, one local union in Baltimore instead offered to pay cash to members who agreed to leave the industry. The Port of New York and New Jersey has offered early retirement programs in an effort to reduce its GAI programs.

Work Environment

Although parts of piers are covered by sheds, many stevedores must be outdoors much of the time, including in bad weather. Working around materials-handling machinery can be noisy. At times, hours may be very long, such as when it is important that a lot of cargo be moved on and off piers quickly. Stevedores work under stress to meet deadlines. Some work is strenuous, involving lifting heavy material. Stevedores must use care to avoid injury from falls, falling objects, and machines. Some workers, such as those in certain supervisory positions, move about fairly constantly.

Outlook

A number of factors are contributing to a lack of growth for longshore occupations, including increased automation, containerization, and the combining of jobs in the industry. Although certain large ports will experience growth and require larger numbers of stevedores, data from the U.S. Department of Transportation reflects a stabilization—and in some cases decline—throughout the 1990s in such areas as revenues and the number of people employed in the water transportation industry. Of course, increasing retirement among members of the Pacific Maritime Association and the International Longshoremen's Union will assure a certain number of new jobs each year. Also, to remedy labor disagreement problems at smaller ports, union officials have devised a travel plan for longshore workers in smaller ports who have decided to work at bigger ports whenever positions are available.

The trends toward automated materials-handling processes and containerizing cargo are well established. In the future, fewer people may be hired for manual loading and unloading tasks and the stevedoring work force will probably be highly skilled, well trained, and will consist mostly of full-time workers.

For More Information

For further information on stevedoring occupations, contact the following unions:

International Longshoremen's and Warehousemen's Union
1188 Franklin Street
San Francisco, CA 94109
Tel: 415-775-0533

International Longshoremen's Association
17 Battery Place, Room 1530
New York, NY 10004
Tel: 212-425-1200

Taxi Drivers

School Subjects
Business
Mathematics

Personal Skills
Following instructions
Helping/teaching

Work Environment
Primarily indoors
Primarily multiple locations

Minimum Education Level
High school diploma

Salary Range
$10,000 to $20,500 to $45,000

Certification or Licensing
Required by all states

Outlook
Faster than the average

Overview

Taxi drivers, also known as *cab drivers,* operate automobiles to take passengers from one place to another for a fee. This fee is usually based on distance traveled or time as recorded on a taximeter. There are currently over 100,000 taxi drivers in the United States. As the population increases and traffic becomes more congested, the need for taxi drivers will increase, especially in metropolitan areas.

History

Today's taxis are the modern equivalent of vehicles for hire that were first introduced in England in the early 1600s. These vehicles were hackneys, four-wheeled carriages drawn by two horses that could carry up to six passengers. By 1654, there were already 300 privately owned hackneys licensed to operate in London. In the next century, hackneys were introduced in the United States. Around 1820, a smaller vehicle for hire, the cabriolet, became common in London. At first it had two wheels, with room only for a driver and one passenger, and one horse drew it. Some later cabriolets, or cabs, as they were soon called, were larger, and by mid-century, a two-passenger version, the hansom cab, became the most popular cab in London. Hansom cabs were successfully brought to New York and Boston in the 1870s.

Toward the end of the 19th century, motorized cabs began to appear in the streets of Europe and America. From then on, the development of cabs paralleled the development of the automobile. The earliest motorized cabs were powered by electricity, but cabs with internal combustion engines appeared by the early 20th century. Along with the introduction of these vehicles came the need for drivers, thus creating the cab driver profession. In 1891, a device called a "taximeter" (tax is from a Latin word meaning "charge") was invented to calculate the fare owed to the driver. Taximeters found their first use in the new horseless carriages for hire, which were soon called "taxicabs" or just "taxis."

The use of taxis has increased especially in metropolitan areas where there is dense traffic, increasing population, and parking limitations. Modern taxis are often four-door passenger cars that have been specially modified. Depending on local regulations, the vehicles may have such modifications as reinforced frames or extra heavy-duty shock absorbers. Taxi drivers may be employees of taxi companies, driving cars owned by the company; they may be lease drivers, operating cars leased from a taxi company for a regular fee; or they may be completely independent, driving cars that they own themselves.

The Job

Taxicabs are an important part of the mass transportation system in many cities, so drivers need to be familiar with as much of the local geographical area as possible. But taxicab drivers are often required to do more than simply drive people from one place to another. They also help people with their luggage. Sometimes they pick up and deliver packages. Some provide sightseeing tours for visitors to a community.

Taxi drivers who are employed by, or lease from, a cab service or garage report to the garage before their shift begins and are assigned a cab. They receive a tripsheet and record their name, date of work, and identification number. They also perform a quick cursory check of the interior and exterior of the car to ensure its proper working condition. They check fuel and oil levels, brakes, lights, and windshield wipers, reporting any problems to the dispatcher or company mechanic.

Taxi drivers locate passengers in three ways. Customers requiring transportation may call the cab company with the approximate time and place they wish to be picked up. The dispatcher uses a two-way radio system to notify the driver of this pick-up information. Other drivers pick up passengers at cab stands and taxi lines at airports, theaters, hotels, and railroad stations, and then return to the stand after they deliver the passengers. Drivers may pick up passengers while returning to their stands or stations. The third manner of pick up for taxi drivers is by cruising busy streets to service passengers who hail or "wave them down."

When a destination is reached, the taxi driver determines the fare and informs the rider of the cost. Fares consist of many parts. The drop charge is an automatic charge for use of the cab. Other parts of the fare are determined by the time and distance traveled. A taximeter is a machine that measures the fare as it accrues. It is turned on and off when the passenger enters and leaves the cab. Additional portions of the fare may include charges for luggage handling and additional occupants. Commonly, a passenger will offer the taxi driver a tip, which is based on the customer's opinion of the quality and efficiency of the ride and the courtesy of the driver. The taxi driver also may supply a receipt if the passenger requests it.

Taxi drivers are generally required to keep accurate records of their activities. They record the time and place where they picked up and delivered the passengers on a trip sheet. They also have to keep records on the amount of fares they collect.

There are taxis and taxi drivers in almost every town and city in the country, but most are in large metropolitan areas.

Requirements

High School

Taxi drivers do not usually need to meet any particular educational requirements, but a high school education is desirable so that drivers can adequately handle the record-keeping part of their job. High school courses in driver education, business math, and English would also prove helpful to taxi drivers.

Certification or Licensing

In large cities, some taxi drivers belong to labor unions. The union to which most belong is the International Brotherhood of Teamsters, Chauffeurs, Warehousemen, and Helpers of America.

Those interested in becoming a taxi driver must have a regular driver's license. In most large cities, taxi drivers also must have a special taxicab operator's license—commonly called a hacker's license—in addition to a chauffeur's license. Police departments, safety departments, or public utilities commissions generally issue these special licenses. To secure the license, drivers must pass special examinations including questions on local geography, traffic regulations, accident reports, safe driving practices, and insurance regulations. Some companies help their job applicants prepare for these examinations by providing them with specially prepared booklets. The operator's license may need to be renewed annually. In some cities (New York, for example), new license applications can take several months to be processed because the applicant's background must be investigated. Increasingly, many cities and municipalities require a test on English usage. Those who do not pass must take a course in English sponsored by the municipality.

Other Requirements

People who want to be taxi drivers should be in reasonably good health and have a good driving record and no criminal record. In general, they need to be 21 years of age or older. While driving is not physically strenuous, sometimes drivers must lift heavy packages or luggage. In many places, drivers must have especially steady nerves because they spend considerable time driving in heavy traffic. They must also be courteous, patient, and able to get along with many different kinds of people.

Taxi drivers who own their own cab or lease one for a long period of time are generally expected to keep their cab clean. Large companies have workers who take care of this task for all the vehicles in the company fleet.

Employers

Taxi drivers are often employed by a cab service and drive cars owned by the company. Some drivers pay a fee and lease cabs owned by a taxi company while others own and operate their own cars.

Starting Out

Usually people who want to be a taxi driver apply directly to taxicab companies that may be hiring new drivers. Taxicab companies are usually listed in the yellow pages. It may take some time to obtain the necessary license to drive a cab, and some companies or municipalities may require additional training, so it may not be possible to begin work immediately. People who have sufficient funds may buy their own cab, but they usually must secure a municipal permit to operate it.

Earnings

Earnings for taxi drivers vary widely, depending on the number of hours they work, the method by which they are paid, the season, the weather, and other factors. In 1996, the median earnings for full-time taxi drivers was $20,124. The lowest 10 percent of full-time taxi drivers earned $9,984 annually, while the highest 10 percent averaged $44,200 a year.

Limited information suggests that independent owner-drivers can average anywhere between $20,000 to $30,000 annually, including tips. This assumes they work the industry average of eight to ten hours a day, five days a week.

Many taxi drivers are paid a percentage of the fares they collect, often 40 to 50 percent of total fares. Other drivers receive a base amount plus a commission related to the amount of business they do. A few drivers are guaranteed minimum daily or weekly wages. Drivers who lease their cabs may keep all the fare money above the amount of the leasing fee they pay the cab company. Tips are also an important part of the earnings of taxi drivers. They can equal 15 to 20 percent or more of total fares. Most taxi drivers do not enjoy company-provided fringe benefits, such as pension plans.

Earnings fluctuate with the season and the weather. Winter is generally the busiest season, and snow and rain almost always produce a busy day. There is also a relationship between general economic conditions and the earnings of taxi drivers, because there is more competition for less business when the economy is in a slump.

Work Environment

Many taxi drivers put in long hours, working up to nine or ten hours a day, five or six days a week. They do not receive overtime pay. Other drivers are part-time workers. Drivers may work Sundays, holidays, or evening hours.

Taxi drivers must be able to get along with their passengers, including those who try their patience or expect too much. Some people urge drivers to go very fast, for example, but drivers who comply may risk accidents or be arrested for speeding. Drivers may have to work under other difficult conditions, such as heavy traffic and bad weather. Taxi drivers must be able to drive safely under pressure. In some places, drivers must be wary because there is a considerable chance of being robbed.

Outlook

There will always be a need for taxi drivers. Job opportunities for taxi drivers are expected to grow faster than the average through 2006. The high turnover rate in this occupation means that many of the new job openings that develop in the future will come when drivers leave their jobs to go into another kind of work. In addition, as the American population grows, the overall demand for taxi drivers will probably increase too; thus the total employment in this field will rise. At present many drivers work on a part-time basis, and that situation is likely to continue.

For More Information

The following association can provide additional information regarding the taxi driving profession.

International Taxicab and Livery Association
3849 Farragut Avenue
Kensington, MD 20895
Tel: 301-946-5701

Toll Collectors

School Subjects
Business
Mathematics

Personal Skills
Communication/ideas
Helping/teaching

Work Environment
Indoors and outdoors
Primarily one location

Minimum Education Level
High school diploma

Salary Range
$15,900 to $21,900 to $28,000

Certification or Licensing
None available

Outlook
About as fast as the average

Overview

Toll collectors receive payments from private motorists and commercial drivers for the use of highways, tunnels, bridges, or ferries.

History

The upkeep and maintenance of roads around the world fell to the reigning powers. However, in 1663, three counties in England obtained authority to levy tolls on users to pay for the improvement of a major road linking York and London. By the 18th century, all major roads in Great Britain incorporated tolls, or turnpike trusts, to pay for maintenance.

In 1785, Virginia built a turnpike and other states quickly followed suit. The very first hard-surfaced road of any great length in the United States was the Lancaster Turnpike, completed in 1794. Almost 150 years later, the first successful U.S. toll road for all types of motor vehicles was built in that same state.

The United States contains more than 3.9 million miles of paved and unpaved streets, roads, and highways. With the wear and tear brought on by harsh weather conditions and constant use, these road surfaces need to be repaired frequently. The building and repairing of streets and highways are funded primarily by state gasoline taxes, vehicle registrations, and other operating fees. However, some highway, bridge, and other transportation improvements are paid for by individual user fees known as tolls. The fees for using turnpikes and toll roads usually depend on the distance a motorist travels. Because their extra weight puts more strain on pavements and necessitates more frequent road repair, trucks, trailers, and other heavy vehicles pay more for using these roads than passenger cars.

The Job

Toll collectors have two main job responsibilities: accepting and dispensing money and providing personal service and information to motorists. Primarily, toll collectors act as cashiers, collecting revenue from motorists and truck drivers who use certain roads, tunnels, bridges, or auto ferries. They accept toll and fare tickets that drivers may have previously purchased or received. They check that the drivers have given them the proper amount and return correct change when necessary.

When handling money, toll collectors begin with a change bank containing bills and coins so they can make change for motorists who lack the exact change. Toll collectors organize this money by denomination, so they are able to make change quickly and accurately, especially during rush-hour traffic. At the end of their shift, they calculate the amount of revenue received for the day by subtracting the original amount in the change bank from the total amount of money now in the till. Toll collectors also prepare cash reports, commuter ticket reports, and deposit slips that report the day's tallies. Many toll collectors have keen perception and are able to spot counterfeit currency immediately.

In addition to their cash-handling duties, toll collectors have a wide range of administrative duties that provide service to motorists and keep the toll plaza operating at peak efficiency. Drivers may ask for directions, maps, or an estimate of the distance to the nearest rest stop or service station. Toll collectors are sometimes the only human link on a particularly long stretch of highway, so they may need to lend assistance in certain emergencies or contact police or ambulance support. They may also notify their supervisors or the highway commission concerning hazardous roads, weather conditions, or vehicles in distress.

Toll collectors also may be responsible for filling out traffic reports and inspecting the toll plaza facility to make sure that the area is free of litter and that toll gates and automatic lanes are working properly. Sometimes toll collectors handle supervisory tasks such as monitoring automatic and nonrevenue lanes, relieving fellow employees for lunch or coffee breaks, or completing violation reports. They are often in contact with state police patrols to watch for drivers who have sped through the toll gate without paying.

In many situations, commercial trucks have to pay more when they are hauling larger loads. Toll collectors are able to classify these vehicles according to their size and calculate the proper toll rates. These workers also have to be aware of and enforce the safety regulations governing their area. Tanker trucks carrying flammable cargoes, for example, are usually barred from publicly used tunnels. Toll operators are responsible for the safety of everyone on the road and must enforce all regulations impartially. Toll collectors who operate ferries may direct the vehicles that are boarding and monitor the capacity of the ferry, as well as collect fares.

Requirements

High School

A high school diploma is required for people who want to work as toll collectors. Recommended high school courses include mathematics, speech, and English classes. These will help develop the communications skills—listening as well as speaking—that are so important in the job of toll collecting.

Postsecondary Training

Toll collectors may have to pass a civil service exam to test their skills and aptitude for the job. When hired, they receive on-the-job training; no formal postsecondary education is required.

Other Requirements

Toll collectors are usually required to be at least 18 years of age, with generally good health and reasonable stamina and endurance. Toll collectors must have good eyesight and hearing to determine a vehicle's class (and applicable toll), as well as to hear motorists' requests or supervisory instructions in the midst of heavy traffic noise. Manual dexterity in handling and organizing money and fare tickets, as well as giving change, is also important. Lost or confused motorists rely on the guidance of toll collectors, who should maintain a considerate and helpful attitude. They should also be perceptive and have professional work habits. Honesty in a toll collector is imperative.

Exploring

Students interested in careers as toll collectors should contact state and local departments of transportation, as well as state highway departments. School counselors may have additional information on such careers or related agencies to contact about the nature of the work and the applicable job requirements. They may also be able to arrange a talk by an experienced toll collector or supervisor. Many such professionals will be more than happy to share their experiences and detail the everyday duties of those involved in the profession.

Employers

Virtually all toll collectors work for a government transport agency, be it local, state, or federal. Simply because of their abundance, state departments of transportation employ the most toll collectors.

Starting Out

Those interested in becoming toll collectors should write to their state and local departments of transportation, highway agencies, or civil service organizations for information on education requirements, job prerequisites, and application materials. In those states that require qualification testing, potential applicants should also request information on test dates and preparation materials.

Advancement

Advancement for toll collectors may take the form of a promotion from part-time to full-time employment, or from the late evening shift to daytime work. These workers may also be promoted to supervisory or operations positions, with a corresponding increase in salary and benefits. Most promotions carry additional responsibilities that require further training. While some training may take place on the job, certain management topics are best learned from an accredited college or training program. Workers who aspire to higher positions may wish to take courses in advance so they will be ready when openings occur. It is important to note that there are few managerial positions compared to the vast number of toll collectors employed—competition for advanced jobs is intense.

Earnings

Wages for full-time toll collectors vary with the area and state where the collector is employed. Salaries begin at approximately $15,900 per year and increase to around $28,000 with additional experience and a good employment record. Managerial responsibilities also increase compensation. Part-time employees are usually paid by the hour and may begin at the minimum wage. Toll collectors who are members of a union generally earn more than those who are not. Collectors who work the later shifts may also earn more, and most employees earn time-and-a-half or double-time for overtime or holiday work.

Toll collectors receive vacation time calculated on the number of hours worked in conjunction with their years of employment. Those workers with up to five years of service may receive 80 hours of vacation. This scale can increase to 136 hours of vacation for seasoned workers with nine to 14 years of employment. Benefit packages usually include health and dental insurance coverage for employees and their families, as well as pension and retirement plans. Toll workers often enjoy the generous employee benefits of working in government service.

Work Environment

Toll collectors may either stand or sit on stools in the booths they occupy. Toll collectors are exposed to all types of weather, including hail, sleet, snow, or extreme heat or cold, but booths usually are equipped with space heaters and sliding doors to keep out dampness and cold. Collectors will also be exposed to exhaust and other potentially toxic fumes—those with respiratory difficulties need to be especially aware of this condition. Toll collectors will sometimes interact with stressed, impatient, or irate motorists and must be able to deflect potentially heated situations while maintaining a peak level of service and efficiency. While full-time toll collectors usually work an eight-hour shift, they may have to work at different times of the day, since many toll booths need to be staffed around the clock.

Most toll booth complexes have restroom and shower facilities for their employees. Some may have kitchens and break rooms as well. Some workers have assigned lockers or share lockers with workers on different shifts. Usually the employee facilities are better when no oasis or service stations are adjacent to the toll plaza. Toll stations have communications equipment so that they can notify state police or the state department of transportation of any emergencies, hazardous conditions, or violations of the law.

Outlook

Employment opportunities are relatively good. While many toll booths automatically accept and count drivers' tolls, automation cannot readily take the place of the personal service and human judgment that many positions require. Opportunities for toll collectors often hinge on economic factors such as automobile sales, gas prices, and trends in consumer spending for luxury items, such as travel. Although most segments of the federal highway system that was launched in the 1950s have been put in place, new roads and bridges will have to be built to augment existing highways. Much of this new construction is expected to be partially funded by toll revenues, which will increase opportunities for toll collectors.

Computerized toll-recording in the form of automatic vehicle identification (AVI) equipment or other similar technologies will eliminate some positions in the next decade, but AVI technology is not expected to make a significant impact on the employment of toll collectors until after 2001. Toll collectors will always be needed to monitor automatic gates, collect tolls, and supervise other collectors. Toll collectors may also be retrained to monitor and maintain this emerging AVI technology.

For More Information

Students interested in a career as a toll collector should contact their state department of transportation. Additional information may be obtained from:

American Association of State Highway and Transportation Officials
444 North Capitol Street, NW, Suite 225
Washington, DC 20001
Tel: 202-624-5800

International Bridge, Tunnel and Turnpike Association
2120 L Street, NW, Suite 305
Washington, DC 20037
Tel: 202-659-4620

Traffic Engineers

School Subjects
Geography
Mathematics

Personal Skills
Communication/ideas
Technical/scientific

Work Environment
Indoors and outdoors
Primarily multiple locations

Minimum Education Level
Bachelor's degree

Salary Range
$34,800 to $51,600 to $86,400

Certification or Licensing
None available

Outlook
Faster than the average

Overview

Traffic engineers study factors that influence traffic conditions on roads and streets, including street lighting, visibility and location of signs and signals, entrances and exits, and the presence of factories or shopping malls. They use this information to design and implement plans and electronic systems that improve the flow of traffic.

History

During the early colonial days, dirt roads and Native American trails were the primary means of land travel. In 1806, the U.S. Congress provided for the construction of the first road, known as the Cumberland Road. More and more roads were built, connecting neighborhoods, towns, cities, and states. As the population increased and modes of travel began to advance, more roads were needed to facilitate commerce, tourism, and daily transportation. Electric traffic signals were introduced in the United States in 1928 to help control automobile traffic. Because land travel was becoming increasingly complex, traffic engineers were trained to ensure safe travel on roads and highways, in detours and construction work zones, and for special events such as sports competitions and presidential conventions, among others.

The Job

Traffic engineers study factors such as signal timing, traffic flow, high-accident zones, lighting, road capacity, and entrances and exits in order to increase traffic safety and to improve the flow of traffic. In planning and creating their designs, engineers may observe such general traffic influences as the proximity of shopping malls, railroads, airports, or factories, and other factors that affect how well traffic moves. They apply standardized mathematical formulas to certain measurements to compute traffic signal duration and speed limits, and they prepare drawings showing the location of new signals or other traffic control devices. They may perform statistical studies of traffic conditions, flow, and volume, and may—on the basis of such studies—recommend changes in traffic controls and regulations. Traffic engineers design improvement plans with the use of computers and through on-site investigation.

Traffic engineers address a variety of problems in their daily work. They may conduct studies and implement plans to reduce the number of accidents on a particularly dangerous section of highway. They might be asked to prepare traffic impact studies for new residential or industrial developments, implementing improvements to manage the increased flow of traffic. To do this, they may analyze and adjust the timing of traffic signals, suggest the widening of lanes, or recommend the introduction of bus or carpool lanes. In the performance of their duties, traffic engineers must be constantly aware of the effect their designs will have on nearby pedestrian traffic and on environmental concerns, such as air quality, noise pollution, and the presence of wetlands and other protected areas.

Traffic engineers use computers to monitor traffic flow onto highways and at intersections, to study frequent accident sites, to determine road and highway capacities, and to control and regulate the operation of traffic signals throughout entire cities. Computers allow traffic engineers to experiment with multiple design plans while monitoring cost, impact, and efficiency of a particular project.

Traffic engineers who work in government often design or oversee roads or entire public transportation systems. They might oversee the design, planning, and construction of new roads and highways or manage a system that controls the traffic signals by the use of a computer. Engineers frequently interact with a wide variety of people, from average citizens to business leaders and elected officials.

Traffic technicians assist traffic engineers. They collect data in the field by interviewing motorists at intersections where traffic is often congested or where an unusual number of accidents have occurred. They also use radar equipment or timing devices to determine the speed of passing vehicles at certain locations, and they use stopwatches to time traffic signals and other delays to traffic. Some traffic technicians may also have limited design duties.

Requirements

High School

High school students interested in a traffic engineering career should have mathematical skills through training in algebra, logic, and geometry and a good working knowledge of statistics. They should have language skills that will enable them to write extensive reports making use of statistical data, and they should be able to present such reports before groups of people. They should also be familiar with computers and electronics in general. Traffic engineers should have a basic understanding of the workings of government since they must frequently address regulations and zoning laws and meet and work with government officials. A high school diploma is the minimum educational requirement for traffic technicians.

Postsecondary Training

Traffic engineers must have a bachelor's degree in civil, electrical, mechanical, or chemical engineering. Because the field of transportation is so vast, many engineers have educational backgrounds in science, planning, computers, environmental planning, and other related fields. Educational courses for traffic engineers in transportation may include transportation planning, traffic engineering, highway design, and related courses such as computer science, urban planning, statistics, geography, business management, public administration, and economics.

Traffic engineers acquire some of their skills through on-the-job experience and training conferences and mini-courses offered by their employers, educational facilities, and professional engineering societies. Traffic technicians receive much of their training on the job and through education courses offered by various engineering organizations.

Certification or Licensing

Currently, no certification exists in the field of traffic engineering. The Institute of Transportation Engineers (ITE) is working on a certification program, which it hopes to implement in the near future.

Other Requirements

Traffic engineers should enjoy the challenge of solving problems. They should have good oral and written communication skills since they frequently work with others. Engineers must also be creative and able to visualize the future workings of their designs; that is, how they will improve traffic flow, effects on the environment, and potential problems.

Exploring

Interested students can join a student chapter of the ITE to see if a career in transportation engineering is for them. An application for student membership in the ITE can be obtained by writing the association at the address listed in the For More Information section at the end of this article.

Employers

Traffic engineers are employed by federal, state, or local agencies or as private consultants by states, counties, towns, and even neighborhood groups. Many teach or engage in research in colleges and universities.

Starting Out

The ITE offers a resume service to students that are members of the organization. Student members can get their resumes published in the *ITE Journal*. The journal also lists available positions for traffic engineering positions throughout the country. Most colleges also offer job placement programs to help traffic engineering graduates locate their first jobs.

Advancement

Experienced traffic engineers may advance to become directors of transportation departments or directors of public works in civil service positions. A vast array of related employment in the transportation field is available for those engineers who pursue advanced or continuing education. Traffic engineers may specialize in transportation planning, public transportation (urban and intercity transit), airport engineering, highway engineering, harbor and port engineering, railway engineering, or urban and regional planning.

Earnings

Salaries for traffic engineers vary widely depending upon duties, qualifications, and experience. According to a salary survey by the ITE, professional entry-level junior traffic engineers (Level I) earn starting annual salaries of $34,772. Level II traffic engineers, with a minimum of two years' experience and who oversaw small projects, earned $41,318 per year. Level III engineers, who supervise others and organize small to mid-size projects, earn annual salaries of $51,563. Level IV engineers, who are responsible for the supervision of large projects, staffing, and scheduling, earn annual salaries of $61,908. Those traffic engineers who have titles such as director of traffic engineering, director of transportation planning, professor, or vice president (Level V) earn average salaries of $72,867 per year. Level VI engineers who have advanced to upper-level management positions, such as president, general manager, director of transportation or public workers, and who are responsible for major decision-making, earn the highest salaries: $86,375 per year. Traffic engineers are also eligible for paid vacation, sick, and personal days, health insurance, pension plans, and in some instances, profit sharing.

Work Environment

Traffic engineers perform their duties both indoors and outdoors, under a variety of conditions. They are subject to the noise of heavy traffic and various weather conditions while gathering data for some of their studies. They may speak to a wide variety of people as they check the success of their designs. Traffic engineers also spend a fair amount of time in the quiet of an office, making calculations and analyzing the data they have collected in the field. They also spend a considerable amount of time working with computers to optimize traffic signal timing, in general design, and to predict traffic flow.

Traffic engineers must be comfortable working with other professionals, such as traffic technicians, designers, planners, and developers, as they work to create a successful transportation system. At the completion of a project they can take pride in the knowledge that they have made the streets, roads, and highways safer and more efficient as a result of their designs.

Outlook

There were nearly 24,000 traffic engineers in the United States in the 1990s. Employment for traffic engineers is expected to increase faster than the average through 2006. More engineers will be needed to work with ITS (Intelligent Transportation System) technology such as electronic toll collection, cameras for traffic incidents/detection, and fiber optics for use in variable message signs. As the population increases and continues to move to suburban areas, qualified traffic engineers will be needed to analyze, assess, and implement traffic plans and designs to ensure safety and the steady, continuous flow of traffic. In cities, traffic engineers will continue to be needed to staff advanced transportation management centers that oversee vast stretches of road using computers, sensors, cameras, and other electrical devices.

For More Information

For information regarding fellowships, seminars, tours, and general information concerning the transportation engineering field, contact:

American Association of State Highway and Transportation Officials
444 North Capitol Street, NW
Washington, DC 20001
Tel: 202-624-5800

American Public Transportation Association
1201 New York Avenue, NW, Suite 400
Washington, DC 20005
Tel: 202-898-4000

Institute of Transportation Engineers
525 School Street, SW, Suite 410
Washington, DC 20024-2729
Tel: 202-554-8050
Web: http://www.ite.org

U.S. Department of Transportation
400 Seventh Street, SW
Washington, DC 20590
Tel: 202-366-4000

Truck Drivers

School Subjects

Business
Technical/Shop

Personal Skills

Following instructions
Mechanical/manipulative

Work Environment

Primarily outdoors
Primarily multiple locations

Minimum Education Level

Apprenticeship

Salary Range

$20,000 to $40,000 to $53,000

Certification or Licensing

Required by all states

Outlook

Faster than the average

Overview

Truck drivers generally are distinguished by the distance they travel. *Over-the-road drivers,* also known as *long-distance drivers* or *tractor-trailer drivers,* haul freight over long distances in large trucks and tractor-trailer rigs that are usually diesel-powered. Depending on the specific operation, over-the-road drivers also load and unload the shipments and make minor repairs to vehicles. *Short-haul drivers* or *pickup and delivery drivers,* operate trucks that transport materials, merchandise, and equipment within a limited area, usually a single city or metropolitan area.

History

The first trucks were nothing more than converted automobiles. In 1904, there were only about 500 trucks in the United States. At that time, there was little need for goods to be transported across the country. Manufacturing was such that the same products were produced all over the nation, many in small "mom and pop" operations so that even small towns could supply all the food, clothing, tools, and other materials that people needed. Today, manufacturing is centralized and "mom and pop" stores are all but gone, increasing the need for a way to move consumer goods to every corner of the country.

In World War I, the U.S. Army used trucks for the first time to haul equipment and supplies over terrain that was not accessible by train. After the war, the domestic use of trucks increased rapidly. In the 1920s, the nation became more mobile, as streets and highways improved. American businesses and industries were growing at an unprecedented rate, and trucks became established as a reliable way of transporting goods. In fact, trucking companies began to compete with railroads for the business of shipping freight long distances.

Since World War II, other innovations have shaped the trucking industry, including improvements in the design of the truck body and the mechanical systems in trucks. Tank trucks were built to carry fuel, and other trucks were designed specifically for transporting livestock, produce, milk, eggs, meat, and heavy machine parts. The efficiency of trucks was further increased by the development of the detachable trailer. Depending on what needed to be shipped, a different trailer could be hooked up to the tractor.

In addition to these technological advances, the establishment of the interstate highway system in 1956 allowed trucks to deliver shipments with increased efficiency. Along with the development of new trucks with better gas mileage, trucking companies now could offer their services to businesses at cheaper rates than railroads.

Trucking today is central to the nation's transportation system, moving dry freight, refrigerated materials, liquid bulk materials, construction materials, livestock, household goods, and other cargo. In fact, nearly all goods are transported by truck at some point after they are produced. Some drivers move manufactured goods from factories to distribution terminals, and after the goods arrive at destination terminals, other drivers deliver the goods to stores and homes. Certain carriers also provide shipping services directly from the supplier to the customer.

The Job

Truckers drive trucks of all sizes, from small straight trucks and vans to tanker trucks and tractors with multiple trailers. The average tractor-trailer rig is no more than 102 inches wide, excluding the mirrors, 13 feet and 6 inches tall, and just under 70 feet in length. The engines in these vehicles range from 250 to 600 horsepower.

Over-the-road drivers operate tractor-trailers and other large trucks that are often diesel-powered. These drivers generally haul goods and materials over long distances and frequently drive at night. Whereas many other truck drivers spend a considerable portion of their time loading and unloading materials, over-the-road drivers spend most of their working time driving.

At the terminal or warehouse where they receive their load, drivers get ready for long-distance runs by checking over the vehicle to make sure all the equipment and systems are functioning and that the truck is loaded properly and has on board the necessary fuel, oil, and safety equipment.

Some over-the-road drivers travel the same routes repeatedly and on a regular schedule. Other companies require drivers to do unscheduled runs and work when dispatchers call with an available job. Some long-distance runs are short enough that drivers can get to the destination, remove the load from the trailer, replace it with another load, and return home all in one day. Many runs, however, take up to a week or longer, with various stops. Some companies assign two drivers to long runs, so that one can sleep while the other drives. This method ensures that the trip will take the shortest amount of time possible.

In addition to driving their trucks long distances, over-the-road drivers have other duties. They must inspect their vehicles before and after trips, prepare reports on accidents, and keep daily logs. They may load and unload some shipments or hire workers to help with these tasks at the destination. Drivers of long-distance moving vans, for example, do more loading and unloading work than most other long-haul drivers. Drivers of vehicle-transport trailer trucks move new automobiles or trucks from manufacturers to dealers and also have additional duties. At plants where the vehicles are made, transport drivers drive new vehicles onto the ramps of transport trailers. They secure the vehicles in place with chains and clamps to prevent them from swaying and rolling. After driving to the destination, the drivers remove the vehicles from the trailers.

Over-the-road drivers must develop a number of skills that differ from the skills needed for operating smaller trucks. Because trailer trucks vary in length and number of wheels, skilled operators of one type of trailer may need to undergo a short training period if they switch to a new type of trailer. Over-the-road drivers must be able to maneuver and judge the position of their trucks and must be able to back their huge trailers into precise positions.

Local truck drivers generally operate the smaller trucks and transport a variety of products. They may travel regular routes or routes that change as needed. Local drivers include delivery workers who supply fresh produce to grocery stores and drivers who deliver gasoline in tank trucks to gas stations. Other local truck drivers, such as those who keep stores stocked with baked goods, may sell their employers' products as well as deliver them to customers along a route. These drivers are known as route drivers or route-sales drivers.

Often local truck drivers receive their assignments and delivery forms from dispatchers at the company terminal each day. Some drivers load goods or materials on their trucks, but in many situations dockworkers have already loaded the trucks in such a way that the unloading can be accomplished along the route with maximum convenience and efficiency.

Local drivers must be skilled at maneuvering their vehicles through the worst driving conditions, including bad weather and traffic-congested areas. The ability to pull into tight parking spaces, negotiate narrow passageways, and back up to loading docks is essential.

Some drivers have helpers who travel with them and assist in unloading at delivery sites, especially if the loads are heavy or bulky or when there are many deliveries scheduled. Drivers of some heavy trucks, such as dump trucks and oil tank trucks, operate mechanical levers, pedals, and other devices that assist with loading and unloading cargo. Drivers of moving vans generally have a crew of helpers to aid in loading and unloading customers' household goods and office equipment.

Once a local driver reaches his or her destination, he or she sometimes obtains a signature acknowledging that the delivery has been made and may collect a payment from the customer. Some drivers serve as intermediaries between the company and its customers by responding to customer complaints and requests.

Each day, local drivers have to make sure that their deliveries have been made correctly. At the end of the day, they turn in their records and the money they collected. Local drivers may also be responsible for doing routine maintenance on their trucks to keep them in good working condition. Otherwise, any mechanical problems are reported to the maintenance department for repair.

Requirements

High School

High school students interested in working as truck drivers should take courses in driver training and automobile mechanics. In addition, some bookkeeping, mathematics, and business courses will teach methods that help in keeping accurate records of customer transactions.

Postsecondary Training

Drivers must know and meet the standards set by the state and federal governments for the particular work they do and they type of vehicle they drive. In some companies, new employees can informally learn the skills appropriate for the kind of driving they do from experienced drivers. They may ride with and watch other employees of the company or they may take a few hours of their own time to learn from an experienced driver. For jobs driving some kinds of trucks, companies require new employees to attend classes that range from a few days to several weeks.

One of the best ways to prepare for a job driving large trucks is to take a tractor-trailer driver training course. Programs vary in the amount of actual driving experience they provide. Programs that are certified by the Professional Truck Driver Institute of America meet established guidelines for training and generally provide good preparation for drivers. Another way to determine whether programs are adequate is to check with local companies that hire drivers and ask for their recommendations. Completing a certified training program helps potential truck drivers learn specific skills, but it does not guarantee a job. Vehicles and the freight inside trucks can represent a large investment to companies that employ truck drivers. Therefore, they seek to hire responsible and reliable drivers in order to protect their investment. For this reason, many employers set various requirements of their own that exceed state and federal standards.

Certification or Licensing

Truck drivers must meet federal requirements and any requirements established by the state where they are based. All drivers must obtain a state commercial driver's license. Truck drivers involved in interstate commerce must meet requirements of the U.S. Department of Transportation. They must be at least 21 years old and pass a physical examination that requires good vision and hearing, normal blood pressure, and normal use of arms and legs (unless the applicant qualifies for a waiver). Drivers must then pass physicals every two years and meet other requirements, including a minimum of 20/40 vision in each eye and no diagnosis of insulin-dependent diabetes or epilepsy.

Other Requirements

Many drivers work with little supervision, so they need to have a mature, responsible attitude toward their job. In jobs where drivers deal directly with company customers, it is especially important for the drivers to be pleasant, courteous, and able to communicate well with people. Helping a customer with a complaint can mean the difference between losing and keeping a client.

Exploring

High school students interested in becoming truck drivers may be able to gain experience by working as drivers' helpers during summer vacations or in part-time delivery jobs. Many people get useful experience in driving vehicles while they are serving in the armed forces. It may also be helpful to talk with employers of local or over-the-road truck drivers or with the drivers themselves.

The Internet provides a forum for prospective truck drivers to explore their career options. Two online magazines—*Overdrive* (http://www.overdriveonline.com) and *Landline* (http://www.landlinemag.com)—provide a look at issues in the trucking industry and a list of answers for frequently asked questions for people interested in trucking careers.

Employers

Over-the-road and local drivers may be employed by either private carriers or for-hire carriers. Food store chains and manufacturing plants that transport their own goods are examples of private carriers. There are two kinds of for-hire carriers: trucking companies serving the general public (common carriers) and trucking firms transporting goods under contract to certain companies (contract carriers).

Drivers who work independently are known as owner-operators. They own their own vehicles and often do their own maintenance and repair work. They must find customers who need goods transported, perhaps through personal references or by advertising their services. For example, many drivers find contract jobs through "Internet truck stops" where drivers can advertise their services and companies can post locations of loads they need transported. Some independent drivers establish long-term contracts with just one or two clients, such as trucking companies.

Starting Out

Prospective over-the-road drivers can gain commercial driving experience as local truck drivers and then attend a tractor-trailer driver training program. Driving an intercity bus or dump truck is also suitable experience for aspiring over-the-road truck drivers. Many newly hired long-distance drivers start by filling in for regular drivers or helping out when extra trips are necessary. They are assigned regular work when a job opens up.

Many truck drivers hold other jobs before they become truck drivers. Some local drivers start as drivers' helpers, loading and unloading trucks and gradually taking over some driving duties. When a better driving position opens up, helpers who have shown they are reliable and responsible may be promoted. Members of the armed forces who have gained appropriate experience may get driving jobs when they are discharged.

Job seekers may apply directly to firms that use drivers. Listings of specific job openings are often posted at local offices of the state employment service and in the classified ads in newspapers. Many jobs, however, are not posted. Looking in the yellow pages under trucking and moving and storage can provide names of specific companies to solicit. Also, large manufacturers and retailing companies sometimes have their own fleets. Many telephone calls and letters may be required, but they can lead to a potential employer. Personal visits, when appropriate, sometimes get the best results.

Advancement

Some over-the-road drivers who stay with their employers advance by becoming safety supervisors, driver supervisors, or dispatchers. Many over-the-road drivers look forward to going into business for themselves by acquiring their own tractor-trailer rigs. This step requires a significant initial investment and a continuing good income to cover expenses. Like many other small business owners, independent drivers sometimes have a hard time financially. Those who are their own mechanics and have formal business training are in the best position to do well.

Local truck drivers can advance by learning to drive specialized kinds of trucks or by acquiring better schedules or other job conditions. Some may move into positions as dispatchers and, with sufficient experience, eventually become supervisors or terminal managers. Other local drivers decide to become over-the-road drivers to receive higher wages.

Earnings

Wages of truck drivers vary according to their employer, size of the truck they drive, product being hauled, geographical region, and other factors. Drivers who are employed by for-hire carriers have higher earnings than those who work independently or for private carriers.

Pay rates for over-the-road truck drivers are often figured using a cents-per-mile rate. Most companies pay between 20 and 30 cents per mile, but large companies are advertising higher rates to attract good drivers. J. B. Hunt, for example, the nation's largest publicly held trucking company, advertised 37 to 40 cents per mile to start in early 1999. At that rate, based on a weekly average of 2,500 miles, a driver would earn $48,100 to $53,300 a year.

Tractor-trailer drivers usually have the highest earnings; average hourly pay generally increases with the size of the truck. Drivers in the South have lower earnings than those in the Northeast and West. The annual earnings of long-distance drivers can range from about $20,000 to well over twice that amount. Owner-operators have average earnings between $20,000 and $25,000 per year, after subtracting expenses. Although some local truck drivers are guaranteed minimum or weekly wages, most are paid an hourly wage and receive extra compensation for overtime work.

In addition to their wages, the majority of truck drivers receive benefits, many of which are determined by agreements between their unions and company management. The benefits may include health insurance coverage, pension plans, paid vacation days, and work uniforms.

Work Environment

Although there is work for truck drivers in even the smallest towns, most jobs are located in and around larger metropolitan areas. About a third of all drivers work for for-hire carriers, and another third work for private carriers. Less than 10 percent are self-employed.

Even with modern improvements in cab design, driving trucks is often a tiring job. Although some local drivers work 40-hour weeks, many work eight hours a day, six days a week, or more. Some drivers, such as those who bring food to grocery stores, often work at night or very early in the morning. Drivers who must load and unload their trucks may do a lot of lifting, stooping, and bending.

It is common for over-the-road truck drivers to work at least 50 hours a week. However, federal regulations require that drivers cannot be on duty for more than 60 hours in any seven-day period. Furthermore, after drivers have driven for 10 hours, they must be off duty for at least eight hours before they can drive again. Drivers often work the maximum allowed time to complete long runs in as little time as possible. In fact, most drivers drive 10 to 12 hours per day and make sure they have proper rest periods. A driver usually covers between 550 and 650 miles daily. The sustained driving, particularly at night, can be fatiguing, boring, and sometimes very stressful, as when traffic or weather conditions are bad.

Local drivers may operate on schedules that easily allow a social and family life, but long-distance drivers often find that difficult. They may spend a considerable amount of time away from their homes and families, including weekends and holidays. After they try it, many people find they do not want this way of life. On the other hand, some people love the lifestyle of the over-the-road driver. Many families are able to find ways to work around the schedule of a truck-driving spouse. In some cases, the two people assigned to a long-distance run are a husband and wife team.

Outlook

The employment of truck drivers is expected to increase well above the average rate for all other occupations. This increase will be related to overall growth in the nation's economy and in the volume of freight moved by trucks, both locally and over long distances. Currently, there is a shortage of both local and over-the-road drivers. The trucking industry expects to hire about 450,000 new drivers each year until 2000 with continued strong demand early in the 21st century.

The need for trucking services is directly linked to the growth of the nation's economy. During economic downturns, when the pace of business slows, some drivers may receive fewer assignments and thus have lower earnings or they may be laid off. Drivers employed in some vital industries, such as food distribution, are less affected by an economic recession. On the other hand, people who own and operate their own trucks usually suffer the most.

A large number of driver jobs become available each year. Most openings develop when experienced drivers transfer to other fields or leave the workforce entirely. There is a considerable amount of turnover in the field. Beginners are able to get many of these jobs. Competition is expected to remain strong for the more desirable jobs, such as those with large companies or the easiest routes.

For More Information

For further information and literature about a career as a truck driver, contact the following organizations:

American Trucking Associations
Office of Public Affairs
2200 Mill Road
Alexandria, VA 22314-4677
Tel: 703-838-1700
Web: http://www.trucking.org

Professional Truck Driver Institute of America
2200 Mill Road
Alexandria, VA 22314
Tel: 703-838-8842
Web: http://www.ptdia.org

Urban and Regional Planners

School Subjects

Business
English
Government

Personal Skills

Communication/ideas
Following instructions

Work Environment

Primarily indoors
Primarily multiple locations

Minimum Education Level

Bachelor's degree

Salary Range

$30,700 to $45,000 to $63,300

Certification or Licensing

Recommended

Outlook

Little change or more slowly than the average

Overview

Working for local governments, *urban and regional planners* assist in the development and redevelopment of a city, metropolitan area, or region. They work to preserve historical buildings, protect the environment, and help manage a community's growth and change. Planners evaluate individual buildings and city blocks, and are also involved in the design of new subdivisions, neighborhoods, and even towns. There are over 29,000 urban and regional planners in the United States; most of them work for local government, while others work in the private sector.

History

Cities have always been planned to some degree. Most cultures, from the ancient Greek to the Chinese to the Native American, made some organized plans for the development of their cities. By the fourth century BC theories of urban planning existed in the writings of Plato, Aristotle, and Hippocrates. Their ideas concerning the issues of site selection and orientation were later modified and updated by Vitruvius in his De architectura, which appeared after 27 BC. The work helped create a standardized guide to Roman engineers as they built fortified settlements and cities throughout the vast empire. Largely inspired by Vitruvius, Italian theorists in the 15th century compiled enormous amounts of information and ideas on urban planning. They replaced vertical walls with angular fortifications in response to evolving methods of war, widened streets and opened up squares by building new churches, halls, and palaces, and generally focused on a symmetrical style that quickly became fashionable in many of the more prosperous European cities. Modern urban planning owes much of its impetus to the Industrial Revolution. A more sanitary environment was sought by the demolishing of slums, and new laws were developed to control new construction and monitor the condition of old buildings. In 1848, in Paris, Baron George Eugene Haussmann oversaw the destruction and replacement of 40 percent of the city's houses with new ones and the creation of new neighborhoods and a park system. In England, in 1875, the Public Health Act allowed municipalities to regulate new construction, the removal of waste, and newly constructed water and sewer systems.

The Job

A planner assists in the development or maintenance of well-ordered and attractive communities. Working for a government agency or as a consultant, planners are involved in integrating new buildings, houses, sites, and subdivisions into an overall city plan. This plan coordinates streets, traffic, public facilities, water and sewage, transportation, safety, and endangered or sensitive ecological regions such as wildlife habitats, wetlands, and floodplains. Planners also are involved in renovating and preserving historic buildings. They work with a variety of professionals, including architects, artists, computer programmers, engineers, economists, landscape architects, land developers, lawyers, writers, and environmental and other special interest groups.

Chris Wayne works as a planner for the city of Omaha, Nebraska, and is involved in redevelopment. His work involves identifying project sites—buildings that the planning department wants to redevelop—and going about acquiring the property. He must research the property to determine who owns it, then hire an appraiser to determine the worth of the building. The appraisal is then presented to the building's owner. The city may have to vacate the building once the property is purchased. "This involves interviewing the residents," Chris says, "to determine what's necessary for them to move. We determine what amount they'll be compensated." Various community programs assist in finding new housing or providing the tenant with funds for the move. Once the property has been vacated, the planning department accepts and reviews proposals from developers. A developer is then offered a contract. When demolition and construction begins, Chris's department must monitor the project and make the necessary payments.

Unused or undeveloped land also concerns you as an urban planner. Planners may help design the layout for a proposed building, traffic circulation, parking considerations, and the use of open space. They are also responsible for suggesting ways to implement these programs or proposals, including their costs and how to raise funding for them.

Schools, churches, recreational areas, and residential tracts are studied to determine how they fit into a plan of usefulness and beauty. As with the other factors, specifications of the nature and kinds of buildings must be considered. Zoning, which regulates the specific use of land and buildings, is one aspect of the work of planning.

Some urban and regional planners teach in colleges and schools of planning, and many do consulting work. Planners today are concerned not only with city codes, but also with environmental problems of water pollution, solid waste disposal, water treatment plants, and public housing.

Planners may work in older cities or design new ones. Columbia, Maryland, and Reston, Virginia, both built in the 1960s, are examples of planned communities. Before plans for such communities can be developed, planners must prepare detailed maps and charts showing the proposed use of land for housing, business, and community needs. These studies provide information on the types of industries that will be located there, the locations of housing developments and businesses, and the plans for handling such basic needs as transportation, water, and sewage treatment. After the charts have been analyzed, planners design the layout in a form that will illustrate their ideas to others who will be involved, such as land developers, city officials, housing experts, architects, and construction firms.

The following short paragraphs list the wide variety of planners within the field.

Human services planners work to develop health and social service programs to upgrade living standards for those lacking opportunities or resources. They frequently work for private health care organizations and government agencies.

Historic preservation planners use their knowledge of the law and economics to help preserve historic buildings, sites, and neighborhoods. They are frequently employed by state agencies, local governments, and the National Park Service.

Transportation planners, working mainly for government agencies, oversee the transportation infrastructure of a community, keeping in mind local priorities such as economic development and environmental concerns.

Housing and community development planners analyze housing needs, studying neighborhoods to identify potential opportunities and problems that may help or hinder the positive growth of a neighborhood and its surrounding communities. Such planners are usually employed by private real estate and financial concerns, local governments, and community development organizations.

Economic development planners, usually employed by local governments or chambers of commerce, focus on attracting and retaining industry to a specific community. They communicate the presence of these resources to those in industry who select sites for plants, warehouses, and other major projects.

Environmental planners are advocates for the integration of environmental issues into building construction, land use, and other community objectives. They work at all levels of government and for some nonprofit organizations.

Urban design planners use their special knowledge of architecture and urban policy to link multiple facilities and the land that connects them into the larger community. Employers include large-scale developers, private consulting firms, and local governments.

Those who specialize in strategies for regional and national development are known as *international development planners.* They focus on topics such as transportation, rural development, modernization, and urbanization. They are frequently employed by international agencies, such as the United Nations, and by national governments in less developed countries.

Requirements

High School

Prospective planners should take courses in government and social studies to learn about the structure of cities and counties. You'll need good communication skills for working with people in a variety of professions, so take courses in English composition and journalism. Drafting, architecture, and art classes will familiarize you with the basics of design. Become active on your student council so that you can be involved in implementing changes for the school community.

Postsecondary Training

A college education—with a major in urban and regional planning, architecture, landscape architecture, civil engineering, or public administration—is the minimum requirement for trainee jobs with most municipal or other government boards and agencies. Typical courses include geography, public administration, political science, law, engineering, architecture, landscape architecture, real estate, finance, and management. Computer courses and training in statistical techniques are also essential. Your school will direct you to internship opportunities with city planning departments.

For a career in planning, a master's degree in city or regional planning is usually needed. When considering schools, check with the American Planning Association (APA) for a list of accredited undergraduate and graduate planning programs. The APA can also direct you to scholarship and fellowship programs available to students enrolled in planning programs.

Certification or Licensing

Although certification is not a requirement, it is a valued credential that often leads to more responsible, better-paying positions. The American Institute of Certified Planners, a part of the APA, grants certification to urban planners who meet certain academic and professional requirements and successfully complete an examination. The exam tests a planner's knowledge of the history and future of planning, research methods, plan implementation, and other relevant subjects.

Other Requirements

Chris pursued a master's in urban studies because he was drawn to community development. "I was interested in the social interaction of people and the space they occupy, such as parks and plazas," Chris says. Good city planners should have design skills and a good understanding of spatial relationships. Good analytical skills will help them in evaluating projects. They must be able to visualize the relationships between streets, buildings, parks, and other planned spaces. They must be imaginative and possess vision in order to anticipate potential planning problems. Logic and problem-solving abilities are also important.

Exploring

Research the origins of your city by visiting the county courthouse and local library. There you'll find early photographs and maps of the city that can give you an idea of what went into the planning of the area. Study the development of your city and visit historic areas. Learn the histories of some of the old buildings. You may want to get involved in efforts to preserve buildings and areas that are threatened.

With the help of a teacher or academic advisor, you may be able to arrange a speech by a qualified planner or interview a planner to gain details of the job in a particular community. Another good way to see what planners do is by attending a meeting of a local planning commission, which, by law, is open to the public. Notices of meetings are usually published, but interested students can also call their local planning office for information.

Employers

Many planners take full-time work at the places they intern. Others look far and wide upon graduation, applying for jobs advertised nationally. Whereas opportunities used to be limited to city planning offices and consulting firms, planners are now finding work with state government and nonprofit organizations as well. Planners work for agencies that focus on particular areas of city research and development, such as transportation, the environment, and housing. Urban and regional planners are also sought after by the United Nations and national governments of rapidly modernizing countries. Colleges and law firms also hire planners.

Starting Out

Experience in a planning office, an advocacy organization, or with a private planning, architectural, or engineering firm will be useful before applying to city, county, or regional planning agencies. Membership in one of the professional organizations is helpful in locating job opportunities. These include the APA (which publishes *JobMart* and maintains an online job database), American Institute of Architects, American Society of Civil Engineers, International City/County Managers Association, and the Engineers Council for Professional Development. The APA offers a discounted membership to college students; the membership includes a subscription to the student newsletter, along with information about internships.

Because most planning staffs are small, directors are usually eager to fill positions quickly. As a result, job availability is highly variable. Students are advised to research the field and send out resumes with their expected date of graduation even before they complete their degree requirements.

Advancement

Advancement takes place as the beginning assistant moves to more inclusive and responsible jobs within the planning board or department and to appointment as planner. The positions of senior planner and planning director are successive steps in some agencies. Frequently, experienced planners obtain advancement by moving to a larger city or county planning board, where they can become responsible for larger and more complicated problems and projects. Other planners may become consultants to communities that cannot afford a full-time planner. Some planners also serve as city managers, cabinet secretaries, and presidents of consulting firms.

Earnings

Earnings vary based on gender, experience, and the population of the city or town the planner serves. Although women still earn less than men in the profession, women's salaries are increasing faster than men's. The median salary for all urban and regional planners is about $45,300 according to the APA's 1995 salary survey. Urban and regional planners with less than five years' experience earned median salaries between $30,700 and $37,400. Those with between five and 10 years of service earned median salaries between $39,300 and $45,900. Planners with over 10 years experience earned median salaries between $52,100 and $63,300. Salaries for planning directors are considerably higher, ranging from $31,700 with five years or less experience to as high as $75,900 per year with 10 or more years of experience. The five states with the highest starting salaries are California, Connecticut, Washington, Hawaii, and New Jersey.

Because many planners work for government agencies, they usually have sick leave and vacation privileges and are covered by retirement and health plans. Many planners receive the use of a city automobile.

Consultants are generally paid on a fee basis. Their earnings are often high and vary greatly according to their reputations and work experience. Their earnings will depend on the number of consulting jobs they accept.

Work Environment

Conditions of work are good. As a planner, you'll spend a considerable amount of time in your office. However, in order to gather data about the areas you plan to develop, you will spend some time outdoors examining the land, structures, and traffic. Most planners work standard 40-hour weeks, but you must frequently attend weekend meetings or public forums with citizen groups, or meetings of town or city councils to explain your proposals.

You'll often work alone, but you'll be required to interact with land developers, public officials, civic leaders, and citizens' groups. You may also face opposition from interest groups representing those affected by your development proposals. Planners must have the patience needed to work with these disparate groups. The job may sometimes be stressful due to deadlines, project proposals, or the unpopularity of your proposals in both the public and private sectors.

Outlook

Opportunities will exist for graduates with professional city and regional planning training, but the market is small and highly competitive. The overall demand for city planners is expected to grow more slowly than the average through 2006. But the growth of the economy has helped planners as cities spend money to improve neighborhoods, develop subdivisions, and expand transportation departments. More communities will be turning to professional planners for help in determining the most effective way to meet the rising requirements for physical facilities resulting from urbanization and the growth in population. There will also be an increased demand for urban and regional planners to help fulfill the following needs: to zone and plan land use for undeveloped and nonmetropolitan areas; to assist with the planning of commercial development in rapidly growing suburban areas; to help redevelop the central cities; to assist in replacing old public facilities such as bridges, highways, and sewers; and to help to preserve historic sites and rehabilitate older buildings.

Factors that may affect job growth include government regulation regarding the environment, housing, transportation, and land use and development, such as the Clean Air Act, and the necessity of replacing the national infrastructure, including highways, bridges, and sewer and water systems. Other factors include the continuing redevelopment of inner-city areas and the continued expansion of suburban areas.

For More Information

To learn more about planning as a career and about accredited planning programs, contact:

American Planning Association
122 South Michigan Avenue, Suite 1600
Chicago, IL 60603
Tel: 312-786-6344
Web: http://www.planning.org

To learn about city management and the issues affecting today's cities, visit the ICMA Web site:

International City/County Management Association
777 North Capitol Street, NE, Suite 500
Washington, DC 20002
Tel: 202-289-4262
Web: http://www.icma.org

Index